T0358235

Routledge Library Editions

THE ECONOMICS OF
REPRESSED INFLATION

ECONOMICS

Routledge Library Editions – Economics

MONETARY ECONOMICS
In 4 Volumes

THE ECONOMICS OF
REPRESSED INFLATION

HAROLD KARR CHARLESWORTH

LONDON AND NEW YORK

First published in 1956

Published 2003 by Routledge
2 Park Square, Milton Park, Abingdon, Oxon OX14 4RN
605 Third Avenue, New York, NY 10017

Routledge is an imprint of the Taylor & Francis Group, an informa business

Copyright © 1956 Taylor & Francis

The publishers have made every effort to contact authors/copyright holders
of the works reprinted in *Routledge Library Editions – Economics*. This has
not been possible in every case, however, and we would welcome
correspondence from those individuals/companies we have been unable to
trace.

These reprints are taken from original copies of each book. In many cases
the condition of these originals is not perfect. The publisher has gone to
great lengths to ensure the quality of these reprints, but wishes to point
out that certain characteristics of the original copies will, of necessity, be
apparent in reprints thereof.

British Library Cataloguing in Publication Data
A CIP catalogue record for this book
is available from the British Library

The Economics of Repressed Inflation
ISBN 13: 978-0-415-31393-3 (hbk)
Miniset: Monetary Economics

Series: Routledge Library Editions – Economics

The Economics of
Repressed Inflation

HAROLD KARR CHARLESWORTH

George Washington University

London

GEORGE ALLEN & UNWIN LTD

RUSKIN HOUSE MUSEUM STREET

FIRST PUBLISHED IN 1956

To

My Son Douglas

PREFACE

THE suggestion to study the economics of repressed inflation was originally made to me by Professor Walter A. Morton at the University of Wisconsin in 1948. Although considerable research has been devoted to the subject of price control and inflation during a war period, there has been surprisingly little said on the subject of repressed inflation during peace-time.

An appointment to the London School of Economics and Political Science in the fall of 1949 permitted further work to be carried on in a country which had experienced repressed inflation in peace-time. In particular, the opportunity to discuss with economists, union, government and business leaders their ideas, problems and definitions concerning the workings of repressed inflation clarified and corrected many original concepts.

The end of World War II prompted many social and political leaders to believe that a different economic order from that existing prior to the war should be adopted. The new order was conceived to be better than its predecessor in that the goods society produced would be more fairly distributed and full employment at a stable price level assured. In the United Kingdom this feeling was expressed in part by the Labour Party and the Labour Government. However, as a result of the workings of repressed inflation, new insight was gained into the virtues and weaknesses of a free price economy. Many ideas rather dear to the heart of the welfare state had to be changed. Old and somewhat forgotten concepts were reappraised and found to have value, even in a new economic order.

The Economics of Repressed Inflation attempts to analyse the operation of an economy when part of the economic system is free and part controlled. No attempt is made to analyse a completely controlled economy, for such would by its very nature have to be authoritarian and dictatorial. Particular interest is centred on the workings of a price system in the controlled sector of the economy with respect to income distribution, factor resource allocation and the elasticity of supply and demand schedules.

In writing this study I am particularly indebted to Professor F. W. Paish of the London School of Economics and Political

Science. He has unstintingly read and reread many versions of the original work and has offered many valuable suggestions and criticisms. Mr. Peter McKenna, formerly of the International Monetary Fund, also gave willingly much of his time and effort to reading and discussing many of the concepts developed. My wife, Margaret Charlesworth, has offered numerous worthwhile criticisms regarding economics and the style of writing. I also wish to thank Miss Leonne Fleury who in typing, retyping and proofing different copies made several editorial suggestions which clarified the presentation, and Dr. Penelope Hartland for her suggestions as to a better presentation of some of the chapters.

CONTENTS

CHAPTER I

Statement of the Problem

THE historical setting of the problem of repressed inflation is to be found in the years during and immediately after World War II. Within a short time of the outbreak of the war the economies of the United States and of the United Kingdom were operating under conditions approaching full employment. To gain control over the large quantities of goods and services necessary for the prosecution of war, it was necessary to spend vast sums of money. If inflation and collapse of the price mechanism under the pressure arising from these tremendous war expenditures were to be avoided, the economy would have to make huge savings. And if such savings were not forthcoming voluntarily, then controls must be brought into force to limit consumption expenditures. Thus price control, rationing and allocation became fixtures in the economies of the United States and the United Kingdom during World War II. Their essential purpose was to displace rationing by the purse and to ensure that the short supplies of goods and services available for consumption were spread equitably among the entire population.

The terrible physical destruction of productive wealth by the war provided overwhelming political and economic reasons for the continuation of controls after the end of hostilities. Outside of the Western Hemisphere many nations had suffered considerable economic damage. Britain had lost a quarter of its national wealth.[1] The German occupation had destroyed much of the wealth of France, Italy, Belgium, Holland and others. Transportation systems had to be rebuilt, factories retooled and equipped, and agricultural lands restored to fertility.

European statesmen, conscious of the vast destruction which their countries had undergone and remembering the experiences of Germany and Austria following World War I, were deter-

[1] *Statistical Material Presented During the Washington Negotiations* (Cmd. 6707), 1945, p. 14. Total United Kingdom losses of national wealth

mined to prevent a rampant inflation from destroying what remained of Europe's economic life. Some reasoned that a return to the free market economy held the almost certain threat of such an inflation. Moreover, it was politically under severe attack from many quarters. The exchange economy had never been overwhelmingly popular in Europe since it had appeared to buttress the class system. Following the war, statesmen believed that it would be politically injudicious to expect the mass of people to accept the free market economy. An inspection of statistics on production, income and prices during the years 1939 to 1945 for the United Kingdom and 1941 to 1945 for the United States illustrates the success of the controls in those countries in maintaining relative price stability in the face of strong inflationary pressures, and this caused some to conceive of a nationally planned economy guided not by the free price mechanism but by government controls as the means of maintaining full employment and a relatively stable price level. Some European political leaders looked to Britain and its Labour Party to erect a new social edifice, whose cornerstones would be full employment and a fair share of the economy's goods and services for everyone, combined with freedom for the individual.

Thus, at the end of the war, there were two reasons for continuing price control, allocation and rationing. One was econ-

---

in World War II were estimated as follows:

	$ billion	£ billion* (approximate)
Physical destruction—		
on land	6	1·488
shipping (including cargoes) . . .	3	·744
Internal disinvestment	3½	·868
External disinvestment	17	4·218
Total . .	$29½	£7·318

* Based on the then official par value of $4·03 to the pound.

This estimate omits private nonindustrial disinvestment such as deterioration of dwellings and reduction of household inventories. It also does not correct for any possible post-war value of war-time capital work undertaken by the government. Pre-war estimates of the national wealth of the United Kingdom have been roughly placed at about $120 billion, so that the loss of national wealth amounted to about 28 per cent.

omic, its purpose to contain the forces of excess demand and prevent them from destroying the economy through a galloping inflation; the other was social, an assurance that all should share equally the few goods available.

For Europe to replace its destroyed wealth, vast capital expenditures had to be undertaken. With the economic assistance of Marshall Aid tremendous strides were made in European recovery. Production recovered more quickly than it had following World War I, and soon surpassed the levels of 1938. However, the problem of inflation remained. In contrast to an inflation characterized by rising prices and money scarcity, there appeared an inflation characterized by a scarcity of goods and an over-abundance of money. Moreover, this new type of inflation threatened to destroy the economy in a manner somewhat similar to that of past inflations. In terms of controlled prices, the purchasing power was stable, but once the consumer had purchased his ration, the money left over had little value for him. Labour came to distrust money, for it discovered that it was exchanging its effort for money claims the value of which might never be realized. Although government controls prevented the price system from acting as the sole rationing agent, they did not destroy the inflation. The inflation remained and continued to increase, expressing itself in queues, production bottlenecks, empty shelves and black markets. Governments were accused of trying to do too much, and the virtues of the price system were critically re-examined. Respect grew for the free market economy. It was argued that the price system was a better arbiter of investment decisions than a government policy board, that production would increase more rapidly if money had real rather than a controlled value and 'incentive' had real meaning.

It was admitted that without controls inflation produced price increases because of the excess demand, but it soon became apparent that inflation with controls also raised prices, since it proved very conducive to low productivity and thus a rise in costs.

An inflation may be termed open or repressed according to the government's reaction to the presence of inflationary pressures in the economy. If the government decides on a hands-off policy and relies primarily on the price mechanism to ration and distribute goods and services, we have an open inflation. If, on the other hand, the government interferes directly with the working of the rationing and distributive functions of the price system through controls, we have a repressed inflation.

The adoption of a policy of open inflation means that prices will be allowed to ration the excess demand for goods and services and factors of production—movements in the price system acting to produce equilibrium by operating on some section of the general public to bring investment and savings into balance. Prices here fulfil their historic function of rationing the short supply of goods and distributing those goods according to the ability to pay of those bidding for them in the open market. We may say, therefore, that the essential characteristic of an open inflation lies in the operation of the price system as the sole rationing agent.

Repressed inflation seeks to prevent rationing by means of price increases and to substitute instead a distribution system based partially on legal controls. As will be pointed out in Chapter III, there are varying degrees of repression, but the fundamental characteristic of all is that prices become only one of the rationing agents. Ration coupons, governmental priorities or allocations must accompany money if the goods or services are to be obtained.

Repressed inflation implies two necessary conditions: (1) excessive monetary demand, and (2) legal actions prohibiting the demand from exerting its influence on prices in both the factor and goods markets. Whenever the monetary demand threatens to outstrip the productive resources of the economy, price controls, allocation and rationing seek to restrain the excess demand from producing inflation. This repression of the monetary demand and its effects upon the body economic form the subject of this study.

The following analysis seeks the answers to two main questions: first, What is the nature of repressed inflation? and, second, What are the effects of repressed inflation on the supply of the factors of production, on the consumer's maximization of total satisfactions and on the firm and industry?

The answers to these questions may be determined by assuming the existence of a free market economy upon which government restrictions and directions in the form of price controls, rationing and allocation have been imposed. As a result of the imposition of these controls upon models of consumption and production preference maps, it is possible to determine the nature of repressed inflation and its effects on the supply of factors, on consumer satisfactions and on the firm and industry. Because of the inability of the controls to restrain the excess demands in the factor and goods markets, the possible scope of fiscal policy is of particular interest. The analysis presents different policies which fiscal measures may pursue and outlines the theoretical plausibility of their objectives.

CHAPTER II

The Economic Nature of Repressed Inflation

THE analysis of the nature of repressed inflation may be divided into two parts: the war problem and the post-war problem.

THE WAR PROBLEM

A free exchange economy entering upon the full prosecution of a war finds that its orientation must be drastically changed. Initially it is an economy geared to meet consumer demand, not government requirements for war purposes. Consumer demand arises primarily out of the disposal of factor income. Goods and services are distributed according to the dictates of the price system, the sole rationing agent in both the factor and the goods markets. It is hopeless to rely on the efficacy of the price system faced with a swelling government demand for factors to produce goods and services which will be consumed during the war, since such a demand can be only partially related through taxation and the sale of government securities to the disposal of factor income. The link between the receiving of incomes in payment for factor services and the disposal of those incomes for consumer satisfaction must be broken.

At the commencement of the war government demand will speedily result in the absorption of any unemployed factors and a severe curtailment of the supply of factors available for private investment purposes. At the same time as this transfer from normal production to production for war takes place, the increasing nonconsumption expenditures by the government and private producers fulfilling war contracts result in an increasing money income for the factors involved. This is further aggravated by the fact that under full employment conditions, in order to induce labour mobility and greater productivity, increased wages and overtime rates of pay are always necessary. If an inflation is to be prevented in the goods market as factors attempt to dispose of their increased earned incomes, measures must be found to induce savings sufficient to equate with war expenditure.

Therefore, the government, having decided that the production of consumer goods is to be reduced to the barest minimum, must curtail the demand for those goods. To bring this about and to promote equivalent real savings equal to the amount of additional factors absorbed for war work becomes an economic problem of great importance. Unless this problem is solved and the government succeeds in capturing the excess money claims in the hands of the public, the result will be fierce competition between the government and other sources of expenditure in a race to purchase the scarce factor services.

Taxation is one method open to the government to remove increased receipts from the hands of consumers. The taking up of voluntary savings by the sale of government obligations is another. However, when the analysis is directed toward real terms, it is realized that real savings arise only when the economy is willing to abstain from consumption. The purchase of savings certificates or government bonds out of past accumulated cash balances is not real savings. Past accumulated cash balances are the result of refraining from consumption in previous time periods. Real savings arise only when there is a genuine abstinence from the spending of present income received. The public must refrain from spending the income created by its current productive effort. By such action only does it release an amount of factor services equivalent in value to that saving. Unless this takes place, all that happens is a transfer to the government of idle deposits. If the government spends these hoards, an additional demand for factor services is thereby created. Real saving out of current income, which is the only true measure of the present income's inflationary or deflationary effect, can be measured only by the extent to which current spending falls below current income.

In its efforts to induce the public to exchange its income for government securities, the government is confronted with two primary considerations: (1) the rate of interest it is willing to pay on such securities, and (2) the public's liquidity preference. Voluntary lending by the public to the government of its money

B

claims depends upon the price the government is willing to pay for those claims. Under war conditions all governments are desirous of borrowing at as low a rate of interest as possible. If the government determines the rate of interest it is willing to pay, it must create that amount of money which will be determined by the public's liquidity preference.

A rising propensity to consume threatens the government's planned investment programme by transferring resources into industries other than those favoured by the government. To the government the ideal situation would be that in which with increased investment financed at a low rate of interest the marginal propensity to consume would be zero and the marginal propensity to save would be unity. As for taxation, under a progressive income tax system the marginal rate of taxation is higher than the average rate, so that with rising profits because of excessive demand and the shift in the distribution of income to profits, large sums will be transferred to the government. The government must recognize, however, that heavy marginal rates of taxation may not operate to reduce consumption in the amount or the manner desired. The form of taxation is important. Increased direct taxation tends to reduce labour's willingness to exchange effort for money and may reduce savings rather than consumption. In turn, the success of increasing indirect taxation depends upon the elasticities of demand and substitution. Previous experience has taught that sharp increases in direct and indirect taxes and patriotic appeals to buy war bonds and increase savings do not produce sufficient real savings to balance the increased government demand for factor services. However, the importance of such measures in a war economy must not be underrated.

If the public is not willing to abstain from consumption voluntarily, an open inflation may become the means whereby the government can obtain the necessary factors to carry out its war programme. Rising prices will restrict consumption in the lower income groups and shift income from those groups to the higher income groups and business, where heavy taxation of the abnormal profits received by the entrepreneurs because of the inflation will reduce their competition with the government for factor services. In addition, their marginal propensity to save is higher. As a result, a greater shift of factors from consumption to war production industries is allowed. The government's power of money creation always assures its ability to purchase the factors so released. Moreover, the use of such power in itself need not be inflationary. If the public's liquidity preference increases and it hoards its increased cash holdings, there will be no increased demand for goods and, therefore, no inflationary pressure.

Factors willingly accept the loss of real income incurred under open inflation up to a point. If they trust the money claims received in payment for their services, they will allow such claims to pile up as they await the postwar millennium in which they can be spent. However, once they distrust money claims, further patriotic appeals to maintain or to increase voluntary savings will be of little use. A fear about the stability of money leads to a flight from money into goods and the danger of a hyper-inflation. This would wreck any government's war programme. The all-important problem becomes, therefore, stability in the value of money. Only with faith in such stability will the factors willingly exchange their services for money claims on a distant future.

In modern war economies, realization of the dangers of open inflation and the limitations of taxation and voluntary savings campaigns in transferring money claims to the government forces the employment of other means. The further step is taken of introducing direct controls, and repressed inflation becomes the means of increasing real savings in the economy. Price ceilings are fixed, rationing is introduced, allocation of scarce factors is made by a governmental agency, investment expenditures are guided and aimed at increasing war output, exports are restricted severely, and imports are increased to relieve inflationary pressure. The presence of controls under war conditions operates to increase the amount of money claims available for release to the government for war use. It also stabilizes the real value of money in which the government is vitally interested if factors are to be induced to continue exchanging their services for savings. This is in contrast to what happens under an open inflation where the government captures factor services by making continually greater expenditures and outbidding the other would-be purchasers. Under an open inflation the increased nonconsumption expenditures are balanced by rising real savings accruing through rising prices—the price system being the sole rationing agent of the fixed or nearly constant supply of consumer goods available.

Repression of the economic effects of an open inflation increases the amount of savings in the economy since the money cannot be used to purchase goods and services. Money is no longer the sole rationing agent. Ration coupons are an additional claim which the purchaser must have to obtain the goods and services he desires. Thus the public's demand is curtailed and the factors released can be transferred to increase war output. In addition, the controlled prices do not allow the real value of accumulated savings to depreciate as in an open inflation. Factors are therefore more willing to accept money claims in exchange for their services, and the danger that inflationary pressure may destroy the government's war programme is postponed. As a result, the economy will be faced in the post-war world with a greater volume of bank deposits and savings in government securities relative to prices than would have been the case under an open inflation. Repression does not remove the inflation; it only refuses to allow that inflation to affect the economy through the price level.

It must be realized that inflation in war-time is the conscious policy of a government in its efforts to increase war output by transferring factors to war production in exchange for expanding factor incomes. Direct controls are the most powerful weapons a government can employ to carry this out. They curtail the amount of consumption and maintain stability in the medium of exchange. Moreover, with the enthusiasm of patriotism the controls are rather more easily maintained. It is for this reason that the greatest interest in repressed inflation centres in the post-war era, when this powerful emotional factor is not a determining one in policing and effectively maintaining the efficiency of the controls.

THE POST-WAR PROBLEM

Whereas the problem of a war economy may be seen as a deliberate inflationary effort on the government's part, the post-war problem becomes exactly the reverse. The government will attempt to restrain and remove the inflationary pressures. The government's aim will be to adopt an anti-inflationary policy, a policy, however, which will not run the danger of becoming so deflationary as to produce a depression and unemployment. A delicate balance must be found and maintained to ensure full employment at a stable price level.

The amount of inflationary pressure existing in the post-war era will depend on: (1) the amount of investment or nonconsumption expenditures made to rebuild destroyed equipment and assets, to re-equip run-down industries, to restore housing and transportation and to produce export goods for foreign markets; (2) the length of time in which the above is to be accomplished; and (3) the accumulation of war savings in the hands of consumers and producers ready for expenditure in the goods and factor markets.[1] The war destroyed one-fourth of the national wealth of Great Britain.[2] In addition to the necessary replacement of this destroyed wealth, tremendous effort was required to increase visible exports to replace the many sources of invisible earnings sacrificed during the war and to finance war-time borrowing. The high war debts of Britain to members of its sterling area were an additional inflationary pressure.

All this meant a tremendous nonconsumption demand for factor services, the output of which would not be available for domestic consumption markets. The problem thus became similar to the war problem, and may be phrased as follows: how best can consumer spending be limited to force *ex ante* a volume of savings equal in value to the investment demand for factor services? An open inflation would accomplish the equation *ex post* through a ruinous price increase. The alternative repressed inflation would accomplish it by curtailing consumption through the use of controls and the maintenance of rigid restrictions in the investment market. Yet the past accumulated savings arising out of the use of controls during the war years cannot be freely spent to purchase goods and services unless a government should follow the policy of gradually relaxing the restrictions and thus activating the inflation by easy stages as production expands.

---

[1] E. M. Bernstein, 'Latent Inflation: Problems and Policies', *International Monetary Fund Staff Papers*, Vol. I, No. 1, February 1950, pp. 1-16. Mr. Bernstein describes the vast accumulation of war savings which overhangs the factor and goods markets as a latent inflation as distinct from repressed inflation which caused the savings.

[2] Cmd. 6707, *op. cit.*, p. 14.

And if such a policy is not followed, greater and greater savings will be accumulated.

As mentioned previously, the essential nature of repressed inflation is that the causal link between prices and the distribution of consumer goods in the goods market and the allocation of factors in the factor market is broken. Any government seeking to contain the inflationary forces during the war period by refusing to allow the price system to assume its rationing responsibilities must perform those duties itself.

Difficulty arises particularly in the post-war period because the consuming public and the producers of private investment and consumption goods refuse to accept the government's solution as to the proportion of factors to be employed in the consumption and investment or nonconsumption industries. This refusal is expressed in the goods market by the pressure of an excessive demand, that is, a demand greater than the supply of goods at a stable price level. This results in enormous profits for consumption goods producers, enabling them to command and purchase factor resources many times expressly against government wishes. In the factor market the refusal is expressed by an increase in competitive bidding for factor services.

It is inevitable that aggregate demand should be greater than aggregate supply in both the factor and the goods markets in the post-war period. In the first place, in the goods market supplies may show a decided drop in the period of reconversion as factors change from employment in war industry to peace-time pursuits and the armed services are disbanded. Second, the accumulated savings, produced during the war by the deliberate inflationary policy of the government, are awaiting the chance to express themselves in demand for goods and services. Repressed inflation sharply increases the level of private liquid wealth, as measured by government obligations and deposits held by the public, since factors have been forced to exchange a great proportion of their services for savings. It is not surprising that there is an increase in the desire to consume.[1] Third, the consumption desires of present earned income are being denied the public through the continuation of controls.

[1] Bernstein, *op. cit.*, p. 4. Mr. Bernstein expresses the same idea as follows: 'The utility of present consumption relative to future consumption rises very sharply.'

In the factor market the presence of an aggregate demand greater than the supply of available factors presents an even more difficult problem, namely, the correct allocation of factors among their many claimants. But the allocation problem does not end with a division of factors between consumption and investment industries. The problem continues to plague government authorities, for the price system not only rations goods between would-be consumers but it also informs producers which goods are preferred. The priority function of prices is weakened by allocation just as the rationing function of prices is weakened by price controls. Moreover, complementarity between factors is broken; this may give rise to increasing costs because a substitute factor may not combine with other factors at the same least-cost output. In addition, repressed inflation during the war years has created excess liquid wealth for the producer as well as for the consumer. The consumer wishes to equalize his marginal preferences for present and future consumption. Similarly, the producer wishes to maximize the income he receives from his different holdings of wealth. He will seek to equate the marginal returns from wealth held in the form of land, houses, business enterprises and common stocks with wealth held in the form of cash balances and interest-bearing obligations. Repressed inflation during the war years fostered a vast accumulation of wealth in the form of cash balances, deposits and government interest-bearing securities. The income from wealth in these forms is nowhere near as great as the income to be gained from wealth in the form of new industries and plants geared to satisfy the pent-up consumer demand.

Thus there exists a deferred demand for factor services similar to the pent-up demand for consumer goods. In addition, during the war private investment was curtailed, so that worn-out plants and equipment need replacement. Inventories are also run-down, and business firms accumulate deposits and government obligations from the disinvestment forced on them by repressed inflation. Moreover, business profits swell enormously under war conditions; the government is the only consumer of war products, and, for this reason, marginal selling costs are greatly reduced. Fixed costs are at a minimum with maximum production, and variable costs are restrained by controls. Faced with this situation, the government must maintain controls over investment expenditure if factor services are to be channelled into those fields needed to implement its overall policy. If controls are not maintained and the past savings of both consumers and producers invade the goods and factor markets, a serious inflation will result.

How serious the conflict of interest may be depends upon the reserves of money claims in the hands of business and consumers and on the volume of bank credit available. If the price system is not allowed to resolve the conflict and government controls continue to dominate the distribution of consumer goods and the allocation of factor services, forced savings produced by the controls will bring about equilibrium *ex ante* between investment and savings. However, for such a policy to be successful the government must maintain controls everywhere in the economy. The repression must be universal and sustained. Should the government practise a system of partial controls to the extent of rationing the necessities of life and allocating factors with the exception of labour, inflationary pressures appear primarily in the uncontrolled markets, that is, the labour market and the uncontrolled goods market.[1]

[1] *Britain 1949-50: A Reference Handbook*, Central Office of Information, London, 1950, pp. 58-9. The controls existing in Britain on the procurement of factor services are listed as follows:

(1) Raw materials are allocated to industry based upon the policy wishes of the government. The best known example of this type of control is steel.

(2) Allocation of industrial goods within industry itself is controlled by licensing the acquisition, disposal or consumption of such goods.

(3) The controls which are placed on production itself are mainly negative. They are concerned with the relative levels of production of different goods. The level allowed is controlled through the allocation of raw materials, equipment and manpower. 'The most important distinction in the sphere of production that the controls seek to influence is the division between the production of capital goods and of consumer goods. This is perhaps the most important aspect of central planning and controls.'

(4) The location of industry is controlled through the issuance of building licences. The emphasis is toward the under-developed areas of Scotland and Wales where a labour surplus tends to exist.

In the goods market a system of distribution of certain classes of consumer goods exists based upon 'points', 'coupons' and similar devices. This assures an equitable distribution, restricts internal demand in the goods market, and facilitates control over prices. Other controls which exist in Britain are on imports through a licensing system, on labour through the Control of Engagements Order and the Registration for Employment Order. In addition, there are an important series of financial controls through the Budget.

As different expenditures on factor services compete with each other in the procurement of labour, a wage inflation appears and wage payments increase as the price system rations the relatively fixed supply of labour among its many claimants. If labour controls are imposed, wage payments will no longer be the important factor in the distribution of labour. Some type of wage and labour control is essential under repressed inflation, for without it the economy is continually being subjected to increasing inflationary pressure and a misappropriation of labour resources out of line with government policy. If wage increases are permitted, the effects will be most clearly felt in the uncontrolled goods market. Increased profits will go to producers of these goods, and their chances to attract labour from investment industries will be enhanced. If labour is to be kept in the lower-paying industries whose production is desired by the government, it must not be tempted by higher wage offers from better-paying industries. The government of the United Kingdom early recognized the need for some type of wage control. In practice, this took the form of an understanding between the government and the Trades Union Congress.[1] The policy of the Trades Union Congress was to maintain a check on all union wage demands on an assurance by the government that the price level of essential foodstuffs and other items would not increase.

The presence of strong labour unions responsive to the will of the government is a decided advantage under repressed inflation. An inflation in the labour market with partial repression in the disposal of factor income in the goods market is the usual form of repressed inflation. Under this system, if the labour force is perfectly competitive, the price of labour will equal its marginal cost and attempts by a government to restrict wage payments will be fruitless. However, in the presence of strong monopoly forces, due to active and powerful labour unions, the structure of the labour market becomes imperfect and the definite probability exists that the price of labour can be maintained below

[1] The official White Paper which outlines the government's wage policy is entitled *Statement on Personal Incomes, Costs and Prices* (Cmd. 7321), 1948. The White Paper argues that there should be 'no further increase in levels of personal income without at least a corresponding increase in the volume of production'. It was hoped at that time that increases in business savings and government surplus would balance investment expenditures.

its equilibrium level even in the face of inflationary pressures. There will be more vacancies or jobs than workers to take them, but the danger of a wage inflation will be markedly reduced with trade union co-operation. One of the most striking character- istics of repressed inflation is that the demand for labour at the price paid for labour is always greater than the supply, since that price is below the equilibrium level.

In addition, the British government, through its Control of Engagements Order, had some control over the allocation of factors to industry. This order placed a fence around the farming and coal-mining industries so that migration by labour to other industries would have to have government approval. The order also stipulated that workers within certain categories and wage limits must report to an employment agency when out of work. However, the government hesitated to use its war-time powers to direct labour into favoured industries and the Control of En- gagements Order itself was used very sparingly.[1] As a result, labour favoured those industries regarded as less essential by the government. This is shown in Table I. The British government desired to increase manpower particularly in the coal, agricul- ture and textile industries, and regarded industries such as the distribution and consumer service industries as already ad- equately manned. A comparison of manpower changes between the Economic Survey estimates for 1947 and actual manpower distribution for that year reveals that only partial success was achieved. As shown in Table I, some expectations were fulfilled and some exceeded. However, none of the targets for the main 'undermanned' industries was reached, whereas the distribution and consumer service industries together exceeded the Survey's estimate by about 224 per cent., building and civil engineering by about 50 per cent., and metals and engineering by about 86 per cent. despite a recognized shortage of raw materials and supplies in these industries. Wage and labour controls will re- strict consumer demand in the goods market, reduce the danger of a wage cost inflation and allow the government to maintain some direction over the distribution of labour resources. How- ever, these controls are not sufficient in the face of a heavy pro-

[1] Allan Flanders, 'How Much is British Labour Controlled?', *Labour and Industry in Britain*, Vol. VIII, No. 1, March 1950, British Information Services, pp. 21-3.

pensity to invest. Direct controls on investment activity become necessary. In Great Britain an example of such controls was found in the Capital Issues Committee. This Committee restricted the demand by producers for factors by denying them the right to issue securities to the general public.

Table I

UNITED KINGDOM CHANGES IN MANPOWER DURING 1947

	Manpower Changes as Estimated in the Economic Survey, 1947	Actual Changes
Total working population . . .	−177,000	+ 9,000
Armed services	−257,000	−327,000
Ex-servicemen and women not yet employed	−200,000	−177,000
Insured unemployed	+ 2,000	− 98,000
Civilian employment:		
Coal industry	+ 40,000	+ 28,000
Public utilities . . ' . .	+ 17,000	+ 6,000
Transport and shipping . . .	− 3,000	+ 54,000
Agriculture and fishing . . .	+ 39,000	+ 9,000
Building and civil engineering . .	+ 50,000	+ 75,000
Manufacturing:		
Building materials and equipment	+ 22,000	+ 18,000
Metals and engineering . .	+ 29,000	+ 54,000
Textiles and clothing . .	+ 70,000	+ 61,000
Food, drink, and tobacco, chemicals and other manufacturing	+ 39,000	+114,000
Distribution and consumer services .	+ 55,000	+178,000
Public services; includes national and local government and police .	− 80,000	+ 14,000
Total civilian employment . .	+278,000	+611,000

Source.—'Manpower Budget', The Economist, Vol. CLIV, No. 5458, April 3, 1948, p. 553.

Further, it was very difficult for new businesses to start, since in many instances allocations were based on pre-war volumes of business. Factors such as steel were directly allocated to industries. New organizations, that is businesses not in operation before 1939, were unable to purchase the necessary raw materials other than labour.

There are several ways in which state intervention can affect the demand for factor services directly:

First, private demand for factor services can be reduced through taxation and through allocation of capital.

Second, expenditure by the government can be reduced. Though impracticable during a war, it is possible for the government to supplement private savings, thereby reducing the demand in the goods market and releasing the pressure in the factor market. The government can attempt to furnish the necessary savings through a budget surplus by means of a combination of heavy taxation and reduced expenditures.

Third, government expenditure can supplement or add to private expenditure. Subsidies to increase agricultural output are a typical example.

By using any of these three ways the state can affect the total expenditure on factor services and operate to reduce or influence the excess demand in the factor market.

The state has four known methods of reducing inflationary pressure arising out of the disposal of factor income in the goods market.

In the first place, there is heavy direct and indirect taxation. Direct taxes take away from disposable income, while indirect taxes increase the price of goods and operate to limit purchases on the part of the consuming public. What expenditures are made by the public serve to increase the overall revenue of the government.

Second, extensive propaganda is used to induce the public to increase their savings by the purchase of government obligations.

Third, government policy toward the distribution of dividends of private corporations can decrease the amount of dividend distribution. In Great Britain this was done by a differential tax on distributed as against undistributed profits and by appeals to businessmen to restrain dividend distribution.

Finally, forced savings produced by the presence of controls in the economy add to the total savings of the community.

However, these do little more than postpone the judgment day. The budget surplus becomes the most important weapon under repressed inflation to fight the excess demand in the factor and uncontrolled goods markets. Controls which would be adequate to repress expenditure arising out of current income cannot restrain effectively the consumer or the producer from spending past accumulated savings or reserves. To place controls on this vast hoard of liquidity or to destroy it by a capital levy may act to destroy the faith of factors and the public in the stability of the money medium; this danger must be avoided at all costs. The British experience demonstrated that in peace-time the consuming public under repressed inflation will attempt to increase its consumption expenditure and recapture a portion of its former standard of living. Post-war appeals by the government to increase savings through the National Savings Programme were not too successful. The British public showed unmistakably that it desired present consumption as against increased savings. Therefore, if the government's anti-inflationary programme were to succeed, not only would inflationary tendencies arising out of present created income have to be combated, but also those arising out of past accumulated savings.

A budget surplus restrains the inflationary pressure in the factor market directly by curtailing producer expenditure through taxation, and indirectly by restricting sales of consumer goods and thereby reducing the competitive power of consumption producers in the purchase of factors. In the goods market the inflationary pressure is relieved directly by curtailing purchasing power. But how is the surplus to be obtained—by cutting expenditure and keeping taxes constant, or by increasing taxes and maintaining public expenditure? It is all very well to speak of the importance and necessity of a budget surplus, but it is as important to determine the right method of obtaining the surplus as it is to recognize its necessity. Attention must be paid to the possible effects of the different methods available for obtaining the surplus.

A budget surplus in an economy under an open inflation would reduce the inflationary pressure on prices and curb price increases. Under repressed inflation, on the other hand, a budget surplus will not act on prices but instead act to curb the demand for labour. How great then should the budget surplus be to reduce the demand for labour by the right amount? Too large a surplus means unemployment, while a small surplus would do little toward reducing the excess demand in the factor market.

In an open inflation the government is far more aware of the distribution and composition of the forces of excess demand which are pulling prices up. However, with controlled prices the government is operating more in the dark. Thus the problem of a budget surplus becomes a nightmare for any government pursuing a policy of repressed inflation.[1]

[1] R. C. Tress, 'How Much Disinflation?', *Westminster Bank Review*, February 1950, pp. 1-8.

CHAPTER III

Factor Supply
under Repressed Inflation

AN inflationary pressure arises in an economy when the *ex ante* or intended demand for factor services (e.g. labour and raw materials) to produce investment goods is greater than the planned supply of savings. In a war economy government expenditures make up the greater part of investment expenditure. Any private investment expenditure allowed during war-time is directed toward the furthering of the war effort. In contrast, peace-time investment is made up of such items as exports of all kinds, plant and equipment, housing and public works, and inventories of raw materials, construction and consumer goods.

Inflationary pressure may be beneficial if there are idle factors to employ in the factor market. It will be injurious if there are no idle factors, for then the excess demand in both the goods and factor markets will force price increases. An open inflation allows this excess demand to express itself directly through the price mechanism; and price increases in both markets in each income time period bring about a balance *ex post* between savings and investment demand for factor services.

If the government chooses to repress this excess demand by controls, refusing to allow it to influence prices, it breaks the link between money and the distribution of goods and factors. If the market mechanism is the sole arbiter of the distribution of goods and factors, money in some form is the only rationing agent. Where the government intervenes, their controls operate outside of and not through the price mechanism, the purpose being to replace the rationing function of the price system with another system of rationing developed and enforced by the government and usually guided by egalitarian principles in the distribution of scarce goods. Under a system of controls one's ability to pay is not the sole determinant of the distribution of scarce goods and factors. The controls do not remove the excess demand; they only prevent it from appearing in the form of higher prices in the goods and factor markets.

Any inflation, whether repressed or open, acts to change the marginal utility of money. An open inflation carried to its ultimate conclusion leads to a flight from money into goods as the value of each additional unit of money diminishes rapidly. Germany, following World War I, experienced this flight from money into goods, and Greece witnessed it after World War II. Thus an open inflation may destroy the market exchange economy through its effect on the exchange medium. As demand increases in each successive income time period into a swelling torrent, the marginal value of each additional unit of money decreases at an increasing rate, and money becomes relatively worthless. Repressed inflation attacks the market exchange economy primarily through the supply side. The doctrine of comparative costs explains the basis of factor specialization in the production of goods. That combination of factors will be employed by a producer which will yield the greatest total output at the lowest possible cost. This optimum combination of factors is prevented by repressed inflation. Many times the least cost combination is not employed in producing a given quantity of goods and services, because the factors cannot be employed in the quantities required to produce that combination. Specialization in the use of this or that factor is not possible, because the factors refuse to offer their services in the desired amount or at the controlled factor price; demand outstrips supply and no additional factors are available.

Under repressed inflation, prices are held constant through controls, and demand is restricted to match supply through rationing and allocation. The excess monetary demand must be saved because there is nothing available on which to spend the excess money. The saving is involuntary in the sense that the people would rather use their money to purchase goods and services. Thus labour and the other factors must accept savings in excess of their rations in exchange for any additional effort. The crucial question becomes: At what point will the factors refuse to accept future savings in exchange for greater effort on their part because of depreciation of the marginal utility of money to save? An answer to this question is sought in the following consideration of the offer curve of labour in terms of effort under repressed inflation.

In Fig. 1, the days worked per year are measured along the horizontal direction and total income per year derived from such

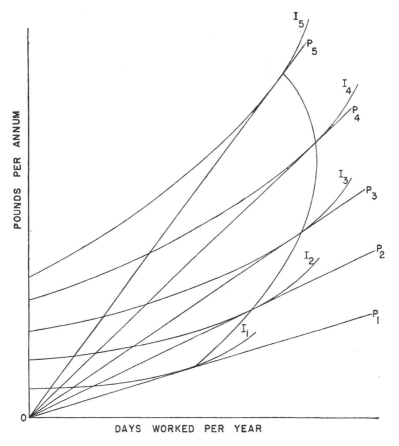

FIG. 1

work along the vertical direction. A system of individual indifference curves is postulated as I_1, I_2, I_3, etc. This system describes in real terms the set of preferences between days worked per year and income per annum of any individual in a free economy. The curves are based on the familiar assumptions

C

common to all convex indifference curves (i.e. convex to the X axis) used for this illustrative purpose.[1]

The straight lines, OP_1 and OP_2, etc., show the relationship between income per year and days worked per year, commencing at the origin. The slope of these lines gives the income received per day. Assume OP_3 is the line representing the income relationship when the wage is £1 per day, and OP_5 the relationship when the wage is £2 per day. The best combination of days of work and income per annum is found where the income relationship line, for example OP_3, touches an indifference curve. At the point of tangency between the two the individual receives the greatest total utility consistent with a given daily wage of £1 per day.

By constructing a series of straight lines representing different incomes per day, it is possible to determine the individual's supply curve of labour. This is done by connecting all the points of tangency between the two curves or lines. The supply curve of individual labour effort is seen to assume the familiar shape of turning back upon itself and is, therefore, a re-entrant supply curve, as shown in Fig. 1.

In any economic system, labour will choose between leisure and income that amount of each which will maximize its personal satisfaction. Under a free economy the opportunity cost of leisure is the amount of additional money income forgone and the goods, services or savings which that income could purchase. Under repressed inflation the opportunity cost of leisure is that amount of additional money income which probably must be saved since freedom to purchase many different goods is denied by controls. Thus the willingness of labour to offer additional effort for money income becomes for the most part under re-

---

[1] Kenneth E. Boulding, *Economic Analysis*, revised edition, 1948, New York and London, Harper & Brothers, Publishers, pp. 742-44. In contrast to most indifference curves which are negatively sloped, Boulding gives three reasons for sloping the curves in this manner: (1) A positive slope is necessary to express the assumption that additional work will be rewarded by additional pay. A negatively sloped curve would show that an individual had no preference as between say 2 hours of work for £10 and 10 hours of work for £2. (2) Since there is a physical limitation to the amount of effort which can be offered each day, all indifference curves become vertical at some point—say 16 to 18 hours. Beyond this point no more effort can be offered. (3) Only positively sloped indifference curves can show the decreasing marginal utility of additional effort.

pressed inflation a willingness to forgo leisure in exchange for savings.

Should labour become suspicious of savings as repressed inflation continues, their accumulation will be looked upon with greater and greater indifference and more attention will be paid to the satisfaction obtainable from taking more leisure. Once the marginal utility of savings depreciates rapidly, labour prefers other ways to spend its time. Further monetary inducements to work have less attraction. The degree of attraction savings do possess for labour depends upon the extent of the controls of repressed inflation. It is possible to discern four degrees or cases of repressed inflation.

1. Under permanent, universal and continued repressed inflation, where all goods and items are controlled and rationed, labour will discount 100 per cent. all income received above that amount necessary to purchase the rationed goods. £100 has been arbitrarily chosen as this necessary amount of income. If a labourer earns £101, he must save the one pound uselessly. If this degree of repressed inflation exists, the income relationship line becomes $OA_1 1$ shown in Fig. 2, where the labourer earns £1 per day, and 100 days' work per year will be offered. If the labourer earns £2 per day, the income relationship line is $OA_2 1$, and he offers 50 days' work per year. The supply curve of labour thus becomes infinitely inelastic at £100 per year. The indifference curves and the income relationship lines above the £100 income level are meaningless, as is indicated by the broken lines. Substitution as between work and income has significance only at an income of less than £100. At this point the elasticity of substitution becomes zero. This suggests that where the degree of repression is universal, appropriate government policy would be to resist any wage increase and if politically feasible allow the general price level to rise so that additional income would be required to purchase the rationed goods.

2. Where the authorities hold out the promise and the labourer believes that savings will be of some value in the future, the slope of the individual's indifference curves, as shown in Fig. 3, will be less steep than in Fig. 2. In effect the individual is rapidly discounting savings at a progressive rate, and this is reflected in his preference map by changing the slope of his indifference curves. Both the indifference curves and the income

relationship lines have some meaning above the £100 line. However, the preference map is much steeper than in Fig. 1 where the individual's choice as between income and work is made in a completely free market. By comparing the points of

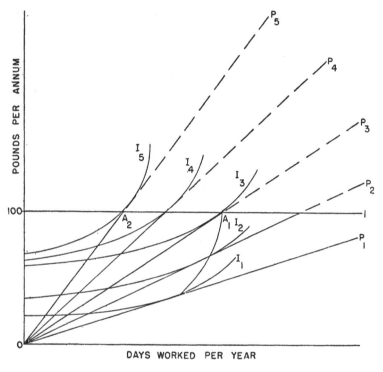

FIG. 2

tangency in Fig. 3 and Fig. 1, it can be seen that the amount of work offered for income is much less. The marginal rate of discount for an individual labourer will be different, depending upon the stock of savings he has been forced to accumulate because of the controls in the past, his income from sources other than his own labour, his wage rate and his estimate of the future date of release of the savings. If savings were a perfect substitute for the goods and services forgone because of the controls, the individual's preference map would approximate the map as shown in Fig. 1 which exists in a free market and more work would be offered for income. As explained above, £100 represent the amount of income necessary to purchase all the goods offered on the market where every item is controlled. The only difference between cases 1 and 2 lies in the individual's

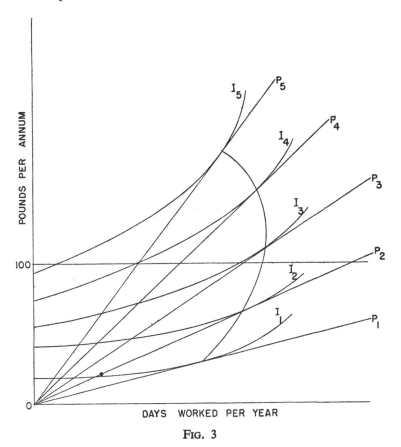

FIG. 3

belief that savings will have some real value some day in the future.

3. Where the authorities promise at some fixed future date savings will be of full value, the slope of the indifference curves as shown in Fig. 4 becomes flatter as compared with Fig. 3. As in case 2, the marginal rate at which the individual will discount savings will depend upon the future date of release of the

savings, the wage rate, the amount of previously accumulated savings and his income from sources other than labour. The difference between cases 2 and 3 lies in the promise that all savings will have value at some future date. This means that

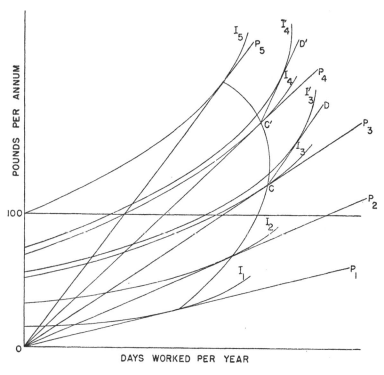

FIG. 4

labour will not fear the depreciation of its savings, and as a result the savings discount rate will have less influence on the individual's choice as between labour and income. This is shown by comparing the amount of work offered at each wage rate in Fig. 3 with Fig. 4. In cases 2 and 3 the labourer commences discounting when his income reaches £100 per annum, for with this amount of income he has offered sufficient labour to purchase all the items he can.

4. The case of a partially controlled economy exists where there are two markets—one controlled and one uncontrolled.

This general case is the one which best describes the degree of repressed inflation which existed in the United Kingdom. The rate of discount of additional income above £100 is less progressive than in cases 2 and 3. The rate is determined by the

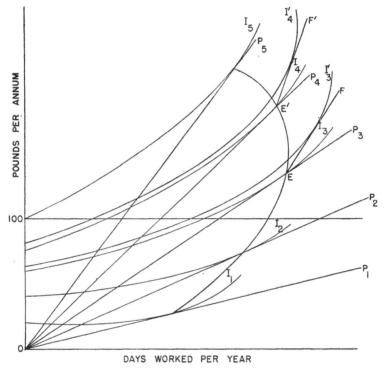

FIG. 5

amount and variety of goods offered in the uncontrolled market and their prices as well as the other considerations previously mentioned. Substitution as between income and work is easier, since income has greater real value to the labourer. The individual's indifference curves as shown in Fig. 5 are sloping more gently than in cases 1, 2 and 3 and more closely approximate those shown in Fig. 1. At each wage rate more work is offered for income. If there exists a large uncontrolled market, the value of additional income is greater than if the uncontrolled market appears in only a few items. This is reflected in the individual's preference map. However, regardless of the size of the un-controlled sector, there will be more substitution as between work and income than existed in the other three cases, because savings can be exchanged for some type of goods or service.

In a partially controlled economy the inflation repressed in the controlled market will add to the inflation in the uncon-trolled market. The partially controlled inflation is by far the most significant from an economic viewpoint, since it is most like the situation arrived at in many nations during and after the war, and particularly in Great Britain. It is the existence of the two markets in the same economy which produces the economic effects of greatest interest.

In all the above cases it is apparent that the individual labour supply curve in each case would lie to the left of the free supply curve of labour, that is, the curve which exists in the absence of repressed inflation and is represented in Fig. 1. This must neces-sarily be so, because in each case the individual is forced on to a lower indifference curve than he would have occupied in the absence of repressed inflation.

The short-run labour supply curve for the economy as a whole may be derived by summing the individual labour supply sched-ules, i.e. adding the quantity of labour hours offered by each individual at different wage rates and under different degrees of repression. The supply curve for a free economy and each degree of repressed inflation is shown in Fig. 6.

Under any degree of repressed inflation the inelasticities and the negative slope of the economy's labour supply curve appear earlier than they do in a free economy. If the labourer's income increases from £1 to £2 per day under permanent and universal repressed inflation—case 1—he will decrease the amount of effort offered from 100 to 50 days a year, as shown in Fig. 2. This is the general condition for any degree of repressed infla-tion, for the marginal utility of savings for higher wage rates will be discounted at a more progressive rate than they will for lower incomes. In case 3, and more likely in case 4, the offer of higher wage rates may bring a positive response from labour, particularly if the original rate were very low. However, the individual labour supply curve rises rapidly and quickly turns back on itself as higher wages are offered. It becomes apparent that as the alternatives to giving up leisure become more acceptable to labour, the slope and elasticity of the labour supply curve change under the different degrees of repressed inflation—becoming more elastic and less steep.

It is rational and economic for labour to act in this manner.

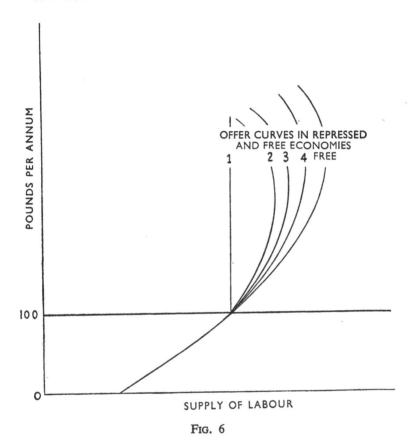

FIG. 6

Each individual labourer seeks to maximize his total satisfaction. If he cannot maximize his satisfaction by exchanging his effort for money wages, which in turn may be exchanged for real goods and services, it is better for him to withdraw his labour effort from the exchange market and put it to better use, for example, by producing foodstuffs in his own backyard or painting his own house. If he does not withdraw it, he is working for savings whose value at best may be somewhat nebulous.

Under repressed inflation, monetary inducements may enlist greater labour effort in some cases. A favourable response may be made to an offer of overtime pay depending upon the rate of discount prevailing on future savings. Obviously, under permanent and universal repressed inflation the rate of discount is equal to 100 per cent., and overtime will not induce additional labour effort. Nor will much additional labour effort be offered where current savings will only be of some value some day in the future, because the marginal utility of additional savings quickly becomes zero. However, it will have some effect in case 3, depending on the rate of discount, and in case 4, depending on the size of the free market in consumers' goods. In each case the rate will be progressive and commence at the point where overtime rates are offered. The rate itself will be governed by those considerations already discussed for the respective cases plus how large an inducement in overtime rates is offered labour. Moreover, it will vary for each individual—e.g. those with higher incomes or more accumulated savings will commence discounting sooner. More work will be offered in each case because the individual can reach a higher indifference curve. As shown in Fig. 4 the offer of overtime rates of pay for case 3 may induce greater labour effort since the individual can attain a higher indifference curve, e.g. I'_3 or I'_4, depending on his overtime wage rate CD or $C'D'$.

In case 4 there exists a better likelihood that labour will offer more effort because of the presence of an uncontrolled market. This is indicated in Fig. 5 by indifference curves I'_3 and I'_4 tangent to the overtime wage rates EF or $E'F'$. Most likely the lower income groups will offer greater effort, since their tastes and wants are more likely to correspond to the goods and services offered in the free market and there is less likelihood that the marginal utility of additional income will become zero. This may not be the case for the higher income groups or for those who already have accumulated large savings; however, as compared with the effect of overtime rates in a completely free economy, labour in either case will offer less effort.

· Since the supply curve of labour becomes inelastic and eventually backward sloping under circumstances of repressed inflation, rigidities tend to set in in the economy. The degree of rigidity is a function of the degree of repressed inflation present.

The elasticity of the supply curve of labour depends almost entirely upon the mobility of labour. Under a free exchange economy the principle of equal monetary advantage operating through the price mechanism shifts the supplies of the different factors from one occupation to another. A position of equilibrium for the economy is obtained when the marginal advantages derived from the employment of resources in all occupations are the same. Repressed inflation prevents this principle from operating through the price mechanism. As the marginal utility of savings depreciates, the exchange economy commences to break down, and labour grows increasingly indifferent toward monetary rewards.

Any condition which tends to induce labour to withdraw its services or to prevent the supplies of any factor from responding to the principle of equal monetary advantage operates to destroy the basis of specialization. Under repressed inflation the producer finds his production costs increasing as labour refuses to exchange effort for money wages. He is forced to use other factors, if they are available. This may mean that the producer cannot specialize in the cheaper cost factor to produce a given quantity of goods but must employ a more expensive factor.

In Fig. 7 the conventional system of product and outlay contours is shown in simplified form. Each product contour, e.g. C_1 C_2 or C_3, represents different combinations of labour and some other factor, say capital, which produce the same total output. The problem confronting any producer is to combine labour and capital in that proportion which will give him the greatest output at the lowest possible cost. Given contour C_5 this position is obviously P, where the total outlay is £175. P' and P'' will produce the same output, but at costs of £200 and £225 respectively. By connecting the points of tangency of the different product and outlay contours, a scale line can be drawn such as OQ. This line shows the most profitable combination of factors for different scales of plant.

As has been pointed out above, under repressed inflation labour refuses to offer OM of effort to this industry—OM being the amount of effort offered in a free exchange economy. Assume that it will offer only OM', because additional effort can only be rewarded with discounted savings. Therefore, to produce the same total product as at P, the producer must combine greater amounts of capital with labour. The total money outlay rises from £175 to £200, and he combines OM' of labour with $M'B$ of capital. Formerly OM of labour was combined with MP of capital at a smaller total money outlay of £175. If the producer

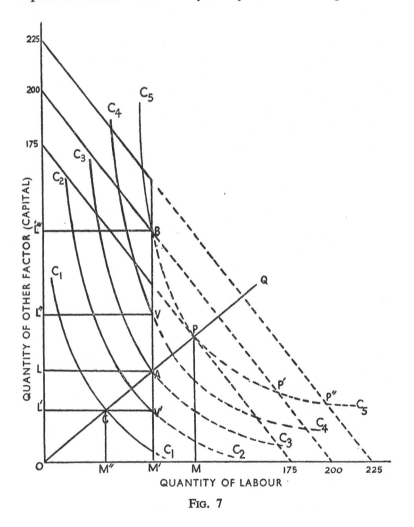

FIG. 7

wishes to remain on his scale line, his most profitable combination of quantities, he must reduce his total output to that combination employing OM' of labour with $M'A$ of capital. Most likely some position between *A* and *B* will be chosen, the exact position being indeterminate, because it depends upon how much capital can be obtained by the producer.

Formerly the producer could combine almost any amount of labour and capital that he wished, the slope of the product contour giving him the relative amounts of labour which must be substituted for capital, and *vice versa*. Now the element of substitutability between factors has been destroyed. The product contours are meaningless beyond the point *M'*. The broken lines in Fig. 7 reflect combinations of labour and capital that are impossible of attainment because labour will not furnish the required amount of effort, and the optimum combination of labour with capital at an outlay of £175 cannot be obtained. Substitutability exists only within the area of *OM'*, but not within the area to the right of *M'*, which was the case with a normal supply schedule for labour. Therefore, repressed inflation forces the producer to produce the same amount at a greater cost, for example point *B*, or to produce a smaller amount if he is seeking his most optimum output, point *A*. Most likely under exhortations by the government the producer will attempt to obtain greater amounts of capital to maintain his production. Production regardless of cost becomes the policy pursued, and the producer strives to reach position *B*. The demand for capital will therefore increase. In a free market this will tend to increase the price of capital. Bottlenecks will commence to appear in the economic structure as the demand for capital outstrips the supply. This may lead to the empty economy, described by Hicks, in the capital market, if the price of capital is controlled without any rationing or allocation of the capital available.[1] If the price of capital goods is uncontrolled, tremendous windfall gains will likely result for the owners of the capital goods. Rationing will be by price, and those who can pay the steep prices will obtain capital; others will go without.

Should the government step in and ration or allocate capital in addition to controlling its price, or should the owners commence to hoard their capital because they prefer its ownership to an exchange for discounted savings, the economy's flexibility is further restricted. If we assume arbitrarily that allocation or

[1] J. R. Hicks, 'The Empty Economy', *Lloyds Bank Review*, New Series, No. 5, Lloyds Bank Limited, London, July 1947, pp. 1-15.

hoarding restricts the amount of capital available to an amount
OL, then the product contours become unreal beyond the point
L in the same sense that they become unreal beyond point M'
as they are transformed into shadow contours.

Under any government it is much easier to hoard or refuse
labour effort than to hoard or refuse the use of capital. To force
labour to give greater effort against its express wish smacks of
dictatorship. However, capital is an inanimate object, and its
forceful requisition is much more easily accepted by society.
Therefore, one would expect to find the owners of capital
accepting, possibly with little grace, monetary rewards offered
for their capital. However, in Germany, under repressed inflation,
monetary rewards offered for capital were declined.[1]

In Fig. 7 assume the area of flexibility now has been reduced
to $OM'VL''$ because of rationing or hoarding of capital. Bottlenecks will appear in the production structure because of: (1)
labour's unwillingness to offer greater effort, and (2) the inability
to obtain the necessary amount of capital to maintain production at previous levels. The essential feature to be borne in mind
is that greater monetary inducements will not increase production. They will only tend to increase the inflationary pressure
which has to be dammed by controls. In turn, greater monetary
inducements themselves tend to reduce the amount of labour
effort forthcoming, or, in other words, to shift the amount of
effort from M' further to the left towards O. Fig. 6 bears this out
by pointing out that the negative slope of the supply curve
appears much sooner under repressed inflation.

The general conclusion of this analysis then is that repressed
inflation leads to lower production at higher cost. The line BM'
is parallel with the Y axis, and any production above point A on
that line can be obtained only at the cost of diminishing marginal
productivity. To move from a lower product contour to a higher
one with a constant supply of labour means an even greater use
of capital and the recognition that the marginal productivity of
that capital must of necessity decline. In this respect it is important to realize that rising costs are the result of the falling productivity of the factor capital as ever-increasing amounts are
applied to a constant supply of labour. The decrease of labour

[1] J. K. Galbraith, 'The Disequilibrium System', *American Economic
Review*, Vol. XXXVII, No. 3, June 1947, p. 294.

effort by $M'M$ may take the form of either a refusal to work more than so many days a week or hours per day, or the practice of absenteeism by the workers.

I wish to emphasize this point again. Whether the refusal to offer an amount of labour effort greater than OM' takes the form of absenteeism or working only four days a week instead of five days, there always exists some point on the scale line where that amount of slackened labour effort can be combined with an amount of capital to produce some least cost output. In Fig. 7 that point is assumed to be A. If, then, we assume that this is the amount of labour effort that will be forthcoming, any increase in production must be due to an increased use of the other factor, capital.

Therefore, the law of comparative costs is less effective in its operation, because output can no longer be produced at its least cost optimum beyond point A. Specialization in the factor labour is not possible, because labour will not supply the necessary effort, in our illustration $M'M$.

The situation which I have been describing fits most closely the case of permanent, universal and continued repressed inflation, where the supply curve of labour is rigidly inelastic. The United Kingdom is more closely represented by the case for that of partial controls. However, this difference in the degree of repression reduces to variations in the amounts of labour effort offered. If OM represents the amount of effort that would be offered in the absence of repressed inflation, then the amount which is offered under partial controls will certainly be to the left of OM. Thus any controls of the type described will act to destroy the value of the monetary reward and increase the inelasticity of the supply curve of labour with respect to that reward. This conclusion has been clearly brought out in Fig. 6. Partial controls will act in the same manner as complete controls in forcing the producer, if he wants to produce at the most profitable output, to occupy a lower product contour than that possible in the absence of repressed inflation. If the producer chooses to produce at the same level of output as that obtainable without repressed inflation, he can only do so at an increased cost. The essential difference between complete and partial controls is one of degree. Partial controls will allow an industry to occupy a higher product contour and produce at a lower cost than that possible with complete and universal controls. However, both of these positions will be inferior to the position obtainable in the absence of repressed inflation.

Under repressed inflation labour is inelastic with respect to money but very elastic with respect to nonmonetary inducements. Labour will obey the call of monetary advantage only if the reward is clearly greater than the nonmonetary rewards. If it is not, higher money wages will not induce labour to shift its job or change the elasticity of its supply curve. Since wages cannot be adjusted to offset subjective advantages, the forcing of wages below equilibrium levels may cause workers to choose the pleasanter jobs and avoid the less pleasant. Labour's action becomes really economic and rational, as even the least imaginative can perceive the limitations of monetary rewards.

It is wrong to assume that the above discussion applies without qualification to all labour, for labour is not a homogeneous income group. The lower income groups will be least concerned about exchanging labour effort for discounted future savings, because normal living expenditures at controlled prices will take most of their income. In addition, if the uncontrolled market is fairly extensive, there will remain plenty of opportunities to spend their surplus income and any past savings they may have accumulated. However, if that market is very small, the relatively worthless savings will affect the labour effort supplied by the lower income groups as well as that supplied by the higher income groups. The size of the uncontrolled market is of the greatest importance in making money worth while under repressed inflation. In the United Kingdom the major disincentive factor of discounted savings appeared in the higher labour income groups, particularly in coal-mining, where the lack of suitable goods on which to spend their income was a definite factor in promoting labour absenteeism.

In succeeding chapters this study concerns itself only with case 4, since it is typical of the democratic countries trying to control inflationary pressures and recover from the devastation of the war. Thus, for the purposes of this study, repressed inflation is defined as an economy with controls over essential goods and factors only. As a result, in such an economy there exists a controlled and an uncontrolled market.

CHAPTER IV

Consumer Reaction to Repressed Inflation

UNDER repressed inflation the government is faced with a dilemma when it desires to increase both savings and the incentive to work. The wider the free or uncontrolled market, the less the incentive to save but the more the incentive to work; the narrower the free market, the more the necessity to save and the less the incentive to work. For the government to achieve its desired solution to increase both savings and work, savings would have to be a perfect substitute for the consumption of goods and services forgone because of the controls.

This dilemma can be indicated in terms of a theoretical model showing how an individual allocates his consumption expenditure in an economy under repressed inflation. Fig. 8, shown below, gives a series of indifference curves, I_1I_1, I_2I_2, and I_3I_3. Each curve illustrates varying combinations of consumer goods between which a consumer is indifferent *in a free market*. The concept is similar to that behind product contours. Each curve represents a given sum total of satisfaction to be gained from different quantity combinations of goods.

As with product contours, we superimpose on the indifference system a series of outlay contours, e.g. LQ, $L'Q'$, and following in the same vein as our earlier analysis, we know that the optimum combination of the goods is where the two curves have a common tangent. If any other position is chosen, the consumer will not be acting as a rational economic being, for he will be putting himself on a lower indifference curve than that possible of attainment with a given outlay. Line OS connects all the common points of tangency between the different outlay contours and indifference curves, and is the standard of life line, similar to the scale line shown in Fig. 7.

In Fig. 8 quantities of goods which are rationed are measured along the X axis, while quantities of unrationed goods are measured along the Y axis. With complete freedom to purchase the

D   49

quantities of both goods he desires, the consumer will purchase
OD of the rationed goods, say meat, and *DP* of the unrationed
goods. However, since the quantity of meat available is rationed,
the individual may purchase only *OD'* of meat. All indifference

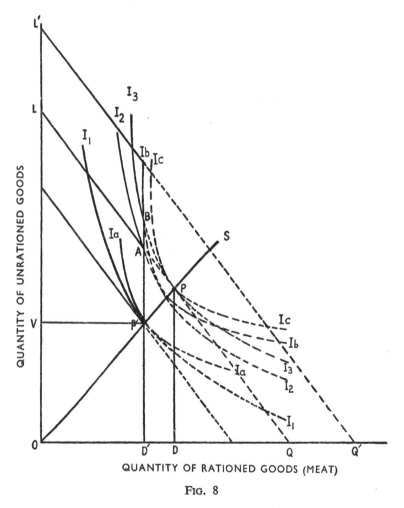

FIG. 8

curves and outlay curves to the right of *OD'* become shadow
curves, since increased quantities of meat cannot be obtained.

The rational consumer strives to place himself on the highest
indifference curve possible. Given the indifference map and

the outlay contours as presented in Fig. 8 and the fact that part of the indifference map is denied by rationing (shown by broken lines in the diagram), the position the consumer will adopt under repressed inflation will depend upon the effect rationing has on his tastes and wants as between the rationed and unrationed goods and upon the level of his outlay contour. It may be that his tastes and wants between the two goods prior to rationing may already place him at position A, i.e. point P and A coincide. There would be no loss in his satisfaction caused by the rationing and no reason to prefer leisure to income.

Again, if savings were a perfect substitute for the rationed goods, the consumer would be able to maintain the level of satisfaction attained at P by consuming OD' of the rationed goods and DP of the unrationed goods. The indifference curve I_3I_3 would be tangent to the outlay contour LQ at every point between A and P, and there would be no incentive for labour to work less.

However, if savings are not a perfect substitute for the rationed goods, and assuming no change in the level of his outlay contour, the consumer will increase his purchases of the unrationed goods from DP to $D'A$ in order to reach the highest indifference curve possible, i.e. I_2I_2.

It is apparent that position A is not an equilibrium position, since the marginal rates of outlay and substitution for the rationed and unrationed goods are not equal. Given outlay contour LQ the most likely effect of the rationing will be to cause a change in consumer tastes. The rationed goods will become more important to the consumer and therefore the marginal rate of substitution of the rationed for the unrationed goods will decrease. In other words, he will offer less of the rationed goods in exchange for the same amount of the unrationed goods, or he will insist upon a greater amount of the unrationed goods for the same amount of the rationed goods. The indifference curves will become somewhat steeper than in Fig. 8 and tangent to the outlay contour LQ at A as shown in Fig. 9. Both the indifference curves and outlay contours are meaningless beyond the line $D'A$. Total satisfaction to the consumer is likely to be less, as compared with his satisfaction gained in a free market, because he has been forced by the controls to narrow his range of choice between goods on which to spend his income.

Whether or not the consumer will shift the level of his outlay contour will depend upon his system of wants between leisure

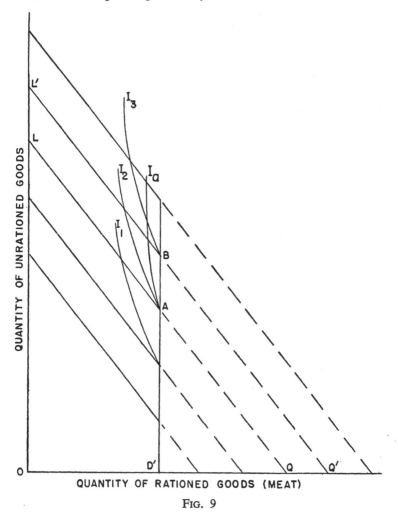

FIG. 9

and the unrationed goods, and between savings and the un-rationed goods. We have argued in Chapter III that the effect of repressed inflation is to cause labour to discount additional money income above the £100 line, and to offer less labour as compared with the labour effort offered in a free market. It would seem, therefore, that where savings is not a perfect substitute for the rationed goods labour would prefer leisure against more of the unrationed goods and more of the unrationed goods as against savings. The net effect of the two systems of preferences would appear to be that labour would reduce the amount of effort it is willing to offer for income and also reduce its willingness to save out of current income preferring unrationed goods to savings. The outlay contour in Fig. 9 would then remain at its present level LQ or could even rise to position $L'Q'$ because of dissaving on the part of the consumer.

However, it must be recognized that some consumers may prefer the unrationed goods to leisure, and they would be willing to offer the same amount of labour for their present income and perhaps even more if they valued the unrationed goods highly. This preference for unrationed goods over leisure appeared to exist among some of the lower income groups in Great Britain. However, it is very unlikely that many consumers would prefer savings to the unrationed goods, even though they preferred the unrationed goods to leisure, since the attraction of additional money to save is likely to be less than the attraction of real income represented by the unrationed goods. This is particularly true where the value of money income above a certain amount must be discounted.

If the consumer's indifference map in the free market is more convex than that shown by the curves I_1I_1, I_2I_2, I_3I_3, etc., the marginal rates of substitution of one type of goods for another decrease more rapidly, and the most likely range of substitution is a very narrow one lying in the general area of the tangency of the indifference curve with the outlay contour, i.e. around point P. This is illustrated in Fig. 8 by indifference curves I_aI_a, I_bI_b, I_cI, etc. Rationing will restrict this narrow range and further decrease the marginal rate of substitution of the rationed for the unrationed goods. The indifference curves will become more vertical as is shown by curve I_a in Fig. 9. Unable to obtain the rationed goods and unwilling to accept the unrationed goods as a substitute, the consumer's demand for leisure will most likely increase. However, as against discounted savings his valuation of the unrationed goods will be higher. The difference between the two consumers one having an indifference map like I_aI_a and the other like I_1I_1 is that it would be very unlikely for the former to value unrationed goods higher than leisure. Both consumers will likely evaluate unrationed goods higher than savings.

It would appear then that the appeal of higher incomes to the individual will depend upon the amount and type of goods offered as substitutes in the uncontrolled goods market. It may be expected that higher income groups will have an indifference map more likely described by the curves I_aI_a, I_bI_b, I_cI_c. This is particularly so where the unrationed goods is an inferior goods. In other words, more and more movies will not compensate for a smaller meat ration. The rate of decrease in marginal satisfaction to be obtained from units of unrationed goods increases as income increases. It would appear from this that the unwillingness to exchange additional labour effort for money income is greater for the higher income groups. By contrast, people accustomed to a lower standard of living may find the goods in the uncontrolled market better substitutes, and their preference map will be more similar to the curves I_1I_1, I_2I_2, I_3I_3. In this instance the appeal of a higher income would induce greater labour effort.

It becomes apparent why the higher income groups such as skilled labour, business proprietors and the professional and managerial groups dislike a system of partial controls. It is also apparent why the lower income groups such as unskilled and semi-skilled labour enjoy the system, because the prime aim of the controls is to prevent income from being the sole determinant of satisfaction. Under an open inflation it is very likely that the amount of money an individual in the lower income strata would have available to spend on goods would buy him even less than the amount he could obtain under repressed inflation, for rising prices would direct the scarce goods toward the higher income brackets. Under repressed inflation it is possible for him to attain a higher level of satisfaction than that obtained in a free market, since the assured quantity of rationed goods at controlled prices will most likely not absorb all his income, and the remainder may be spent in the uncontrolled market as he pleases. Many of the amenities he receives now he has never been able to afford in the past and could not have afforded in the presence of an open inflation. Unfortunately, this happy state of affairs may not be possible for the higher income groups.

The excess demand for the unrationed goods spilling over from the controlled market will increase prices in the free market. If controls are extended, the area of the free market is narrowed and the danger that the marginal utility of money to all income groups will decrease is enhanced. For example, in Fig. 8, if the quantity of unrationed goods is now restricted to OV for the consumer, all indifference and outlay curves become shadow curves above the line VP'.

In addition to their effect on consumer satisfaction, controls act to destroy 'consumer surplus', which, by definition, 'represents the difference between what a consumer pays when there is a flat rate for all quantities and the maximum amount which can be extracted from him by skilful pricing'.[1] The controlled price is a flat rate price, but rationing refuses to allow the consumer to purchase at that price as much of the goods as he desires. Purchasers receive some 'consumer surplus', but not the quantity they would have received had the market been free and had they been able to purchase all that they desired.

The purpose of controls in the goods market under repressed inflation is twofold: (1) to force a volume of savings equal to the investment demand for factor services, and (2) to restrain social inequalities from developing as they would under an uncontrolled inflation which shifts real income from labour to profits.

Experience has shown that controls work more effectively in accomplishing the second purpose than the first. Repressed inflation seeks to lower the propensity to consume, while the public insists on protecting its real standard of living in peacetime by spending its excess income as well as its past savings in the uncontrolled markets.

This tendency on the part of the public to shift the consumption function upwards, when the express purpose of repressed inflation is to shift it in the opposite direction, may be attributed in part to the following: (1) the fact that the marginal utility of money to save is less and declines more rapidly in a controlled economy than in a free economy not subject to an open infla-

[1] Kenneth E. Boulding, *Economic Analysis*, New York and London, Harper & Brothers, Publishers, 1941, p. 549.

tion; (2) the rise in prices in the uncontrolled goods market; (3) the public's attempt to maintain its level of consumption by spending present as well as past income on the substitute goods; (4) the security offered to the lower income groups by the assurance that they will always be able to purchase the controlled goods; (5) the prevention of a shift in money income toward the higher income groups whose propensity to save is higher.

It is important to realize that under repressed inflation present satisfactions are likely to be worth more to the general public than discounted savings, and that the insistence upon dissaving or the demand for higher incomes means that labour is attempting to achieve that higher level of satisfaction which its income would have purchased in a free economy given the controlled level of prices. Thus controls operating in an economy with a fairly large uncontrolled market will prove relatively ineffective in lowering the propensity to consume and reducing the ability of the uncontrolled goods producers to increase their competitive bidding for scarce factor services.

Demands for higher wages on the part of labour must be refused under repressed inflation if the government's agreed-upon distribution of factor services and the prevention of inflation in the goods markets are to be attained. This is hard to do, since increasing costs will raise prices in both the controlled and uncontrolled goods markets, and the excess demand spilling over from the controlled market will further increase prices in the free market. This would provide labour with another good reason for demanding wage increases. Since wages are maintained at a price below equilibrium level, the government can only prevent wage increases by increasing its subsidies to absorb the additional costs so as to allow the workers' incomes to cover the purchase of the controlled items. Increasing subsidy payments to offset rising costs became a heavy expenditure item in the British budget. If controls are extended, the area of the free market is narrowed and the danger that the marginal utility to save will further depreciate is enhanced if consumers expect such controls to continue indefinitely or be still further extended. To control the level of wages became increasingly difficult for the Labour government, and many times the government was forced to rely on labour's political loyalty to the party and to the unions to prevent the workers from striking.

The system of controls of repressed inflation plus heavy taxation tends to equalize the distribution of real income. If the taxes are heavy and social benefits are many, there may be a shift in real income toward the lower income groups. Under an open inflation real income would shift from labour to profits. Repressed inflation hampers this tendency. Price stability is maintained in the controlled market, and rationing reduces the excess demand to the level of available supplies. The workers' incomes are not destroyed through increasing prices in the controlled market, and by substitution many are able to obtain a higher level of satisfaction than that possible in a free market with rising prices. Thus, although the controls may not succeed in reducing the propensity to consume, they do tend to remove social inequalities, at least to the extent of raising the standard of living of the lower income groups and protecting it against transference to profits. If repressed inflation is to work with any modicum of efficiency, the only possible outcome is a reduction in the standard of living of the higher income groups, since worker satisfactions are more important to the success of the controls than those of the higher income groups. If worker satisfactions are maintained, the chances are lessened that the economy will be threatened with a wage-cost spiral. Furthermore, the attractions of employment in the free market are reduced, which will allow the government to attain its desired factor distribution in the factor market.

As already pointed out, the satisfactions of the higher income groups are not so easily satisfied with the goods and services in the uncontrolled market. Such attractions as social position and the power and influence of management together with loyalty to a particular firm or profession may likely outweigh the unattractiveness of money income under repressed inflation and may induce the same willingness to offer effort as before.

CHAPTER V

Factor Allocation under Repressed Inflation

As has been pointed out already in Chapter II, repressed inflation can be viewed as a conflict between government policy and consumer wishes as to the distribution of factor services. If the government succeeds in pursuing its investment policy, it must control not only the volume of savings but also the distribution of factors within the economy. If the price system determines the distribution of raw materials and labour, the government's planned investment programme could likely not eventuate. Labour would tend to move toward better-paying industries, and the raw materials would be sold to the highest bidder. In many instances it would only be coincidence if the industry which could and would pay the better wages and raw materials prices was also one favoured by the government. As pointed out in Chapter II, the ineffectual labour controls in Great Britain did not promote the desired distribution of that factor.

The tremendous demand for factors in both the controlled and uncontrolled markets arose primarily from the vast liquid reserves accumulated under repressed inflation during the war years and the high profits of current income time periods in the post-war years. It seems strange that under repressed inflation business should be making large profits particularly in the controlled market, since large profits are more familiarly associated with rising prices and an open inflation. The reason for these high profits lies in the fact that under a controlled market marginal selling costs are greatly reduced and both fixed and variable costs are held down. When a firm faces a perfect market, there is no reason to incur selling costs, since it can sell all it wants at the market price. This is the situation in the controlled market. The controlled price is below its equilibrium level; otherwise it would not be controlled. At a market price below equilibrium level, a producer can sell all that he can produce, since demand outstrips supply. Also, fixed costs are at a minimum where the firm is producing at capacity output and factor prices are controlled by government regulation. It is not surprising that business profits, if retained as business savings, may be looked upon with some favour by the government, since allying business savings with a government surplus will help to produce savings equal to the investment demand for factor services.

The factor demand arising from the uncontrolled market increases the pressure on the scarce factors and heightens the chance of bottlenecks occurring in the supply of factors. As shown in Chapter IV, the uncontrolled market will be swamped with such a heavy excess demand that sellers will seek every possible way to circumvent the factor controls. Thus the government's ability to maintain its desired distribution of factors between the two groups of industries will be reduced. Moreover, in the face of rising prices in the uncontrolled goods market and rising costs pushing prices up in both the controlled and uncontrolled markets, unions are likely to demand higher wages, particularly if their members feel that any wage contract should include some recognition of the high prices found in the uncontrolled market. This could lead to a wage-price spiral.

In addition to the heavy demand for factor services arising in both markets from the latent inflation and high profits, there will be an additional demand for uncontrolled factors to substitute for labour. As pointed out in Chapter IV and illustrated in Fig. 7, producers unable to obtain OM of labour will seek to substitute capital for labour if they wish to reach their previous product contour. Demand for capital would then rise from MP to $M'B$. Therefore, if the government is to achieve its purpose of maintaining production in favoured industries, controls over the distribution of factors and over the payments made to those factors must be instituted and maintained.

The most usual manner of re-equating demand to supply of a factor is to ration or allocate the factor concerned. Assume that the allocation of the factor to firm A for which there is an abnormal demand, say capital, would be OL, as shown in Fig. 7. OL is the amount required for least cost output on product contour C_3. It follows that all of firm A's product contours above line LA become shadow contours, since it is impossible for this firm to achieve an increase in output by substituting capital for labour, as was discussed in Chapter III.

Assume the allocation of capital to be OL'. The firm cannot attain an output equal to contour C_3 because labour will only offer OM' of effort. The least cost optimum would be OL' of capital with OM'' of labour. Since the firm will most likely strive to increase its output to the maximum, it will combine all its labour OM' with OL' of capital. Increased costs of production will arise because more labour is being used with this allocation of capital than should be to obtain the least cost optimum. Output would increase and costs per unit decrease if the firm could increase its capital allocation to OL.

If capital allocation amounted to OL'', the firm could increase its output to that measured by contour C_4. Here output would increase, but so would costs, because of capital's diminished productivity. If capital allocation amounted to OL''', output would be greater, but costs would rise even more sharply as capital's productivity diminished rapidly.

Low labour productivity due to the lack of other factors to work with was apparent in many industries in Great Britain in 1947. Labour was hoarded by its various employers and inducements even offered to labour to keep it idle but attached to a particular firm or industry in the hope that an increased allocation of other factors or raw materials might be made at a future date. Under repressed inflation we have seen that the supply curve of labour tends to become more inelastic. The employer's willingness to support idle labour adds another element to increase that inelasticity. The employers have no need to fear a drop in sales since repressed inflation creates and maintains a seller's market for them.

Firms further along in the chain of production face the possibility of shortages of raw materials or goods in process due to the lack of optimum combination of factors in the earlier stages of production. If there is a shortage of steel for automobile manufacture, the basic reason is a shortage of the factors of production to produce steel. Thus one of the clearest and most important characteristics of repressed inflation is the appearance of bottlenecks in production. Because demand is greater than supply at the controlled price, some demands must go unsatisfied. The government must distribute factors according to its policy since the price system is deprived of its rationing function.

Where government allocation determines the distribution of

scarce factors in place of the price system, it is easy to visualize the possibility of the rapid growth of one industry and the starvation of another. Allocation is primarily designed to assure that the price mechanism will not be the sole arbiter in deciding the distribution of scarce factors, because it is feared that rationing through the price system would produce great distortions in the productive structure of the economy. However, it is altogether possible that allocations may produce distortions in the economy just as are produced by the price system in an open inflation. For example, it is possible that a favoured industry can be maintained in the face of foreign competition.

The great danger in allocating scarce factors is that the distribution agreed upon may be one at odds with the real economic forces operating within and without the economy. If prices are controlled for many goods, it is impossible to use prices as an index for determining how much of the scarce factor services should be allocated to this or that industry. It is possible to determine that a shortage exists of certain goods, but it is impossible to determine how great that shortage is, since prices, which normally dictate the amount of expansion needed between different firms and industries, are not allowed to express the underlying demand and supply relationships. Controls, therefore, must perform the functions of the free price system. They must choose as between firms and industries which are to receive factors at all, and in what proportions they are to be allocated. As compared with the subtleties of the price system in performing these functions, repressed inflation is not only clumsy and slow but it also tends to increase rigidities in the economy and permit the production of unwanted goods to be continued.

It is necessary to realize how important this problem is under repressed inflation. The consumer seeking to maximize his total satisfactions in a partially controlled economy may force the application of controls on other goods. His field of choice is then further restricted and his demand channelled into other areas. In his effort to substitute other goods for those denied him, his ultimate choice is always between accepting substitutes or withholding his money and saving it.

The increased internal demand for unrationed goods created by repressed inflation will more than likely be sufficient to clear the market and thus seem to support an increased factor allocation to those industries. But this is not the main problem. The main problem is: Will consumer demand support increased production and costs in the uncontrolled industries when the consumers can purchase as much of the controlled goods—e.g. meat—as they desire? In other words, the demand pattern created by restricting consumer choice may be altogether different from the demand pattern which will appear when all controls are lifted.

Any misallocation of factors which has occurred becomes apparent with the easing of controls and the widening of the uncontrolled market. Assume automobiles have been severely rationed in the home market of the economy. Should a slump in foreign purchases appear, the demand for automobiles can easily be maintained by rescinding the controls on home purchases. However, it is possible that the purchasing of cars will lessen the demand for other goods. Redundant factors may appear in some of the other industries. Therefore, the shift in the internal demand may reveal a productive structure out of step with economic reality. The producers in the firms where factors have become redundant were creating an excess supply, though unaware of it at the time. During their expansion period their claim upon scarce factors seemingly was justified, either because of higher prices offered to factors or because of convincing arguments to the officials in charge of allocation. With the appearance of greater supplies of rationed goods, however, their goods suddenly become unwanted. Investment in these industries has been carried beyond the economic optimum, and factors have been used for which there was a greater economic need elsewhere.

It is inevitable that such results should appear, since it is always difficult to forecast accurately the extent, intensity and nature of consumer demand, and it is even more difficult when the demand is controlled. Any producer expanding his productive facilities under repressed inflation should recognize that with the return of normal supplies of the rationed goods his particular demand curve may be greatly changed. Whether the new demand will be sufficient to cover his costs cannot be determined.

The government in a partially controlled economy can play with the restricted consumer demand much as an organist plays with the bellows of an organ. As a pipe organ is played through the release of controlled air pressure upon reeds fastened in the pipes, so the excess monetary demand can be played upon the economy through the release of certain controls. Unfortunately, the tune played by the government may have some discords. In addition to the possibility of redundancy being hidden in the economy by the indirect effects of the controls, there is the consideration that repressed inflation of itself acts to delay many industries from facing up to economic reality. If textiles, for example, cannot be sold in foreign markets because of high export prices, they can be in the home market, since greater import controls under repressed inflation reduce the competitiveness of cheaper import goods. Therefore, why reduce prices or strive to lessen costs to bring the cost and sales structure into line with that of foreign competitors in the domestic or overseas market? The internal market is a safe haven into which no foreign competitor can venture and on which no troubled winds blow. The fact that some industries in Great Britain have been cost conscious is no credit to repressed inflation, but instead is a credit to the industries concerned. There is no question that economically repressed inflation creates the safe haven for high-cost producers.

The tremendous levelling of personal money and real income which is brought about by the controls must be reflected in the productive pattern of the economy once its full effect is allowed to express itself. This change in the internal demand structure may be a good thing or a bad thing. It is good socially in the upgrading of the poorer sections of society, and economically through the attempts by industry to increase production to the level where the greatly increased demand of the lower income groups can be supplied. Cheaply mass-produced goods are stressed both during and after repressed inflation, and quality production is underemphasized from the viewpoint of the internal market.

One of the lasting effects of repressed inflation is to compress the total demand into narrow limits. Total consumer demand may be the same or even greater, but the expression of that demand is confined to narrower segments than would be the case in a free economy. Whether this is good or bad, only history will be able to answer.

In summary, controls in the factor market necessary to restrain inflationary pressure and secure the allocation of factors desired by government policy may easily produce a productive structure at variance with the true and unrestricted demand of both home and foreign buyers. As long as controls are maintained in the domestic goods market, this misallocation of factors will not be evident, since the market will purchase any goods that appear. Another important possibility is that the excess demand in the factor market tends to create production bottlenecks, since controlled prices are below equilibrium level; this creates a cost-induced inflation.

CHAPTER VI

The Industry under Repressed Inflation

IT is now possible to combine the conclusions of the previous three chapters into a discussion of the economic effects of repressed inflation on an industry.

The effects on an industry can best be discussed by considering first the effects on the supply curve of the industry. As pointed out in Chapters III and V, the use of allocations and other controls to obtain the pattern of desired factor distribution results in an increase in costs to the individual firm. Since the supply curve of the industry is the sum of the marginal cost curves of the firms making up the industry, any increase in costs would cause the industry's supply curve to shift toward the left. The reasons for this are: (1) the inelasticity of the supply curve of labour with respect to monetary inducements; (2) the necessity of substituting other less productive factors for labour if total production is to be maintained; (3) the growing presence of bottlenecks because of the inability to obtain factors; (4) an increase in fixed costs per unit because optimum production is many times unobtainable; and (5) a rise in wage rates as union and non-union labour seek to maintain some set standard of living. All these elements, in varying degrees dependent upon the industry concerned, tend to retard production and push costs up in both controlled and uncontrolled industries.

Factor controls also influence the elasticity of an industry's supply schedule. The supply curve of labour is more inelastic under repressed inflation than it is in a free economy, and the degree of variability of the proportions in which factor services can be employed is restricted. As a result in the factor market the supply schedules show greater inelasticity than they would if the economy were completely free. This is represented in Fig. 10 by the supply curve $S'S''$. The broken line curve $S'S'$ shows the shape of the supply curve in the absence of repressed inflation.

The basic determinants of any individual's demand schedule for particular goods are his preferences and wants, his money income and the prices of substitute goods. A change in any one of these three tends to shift his demand to the left or to the right,

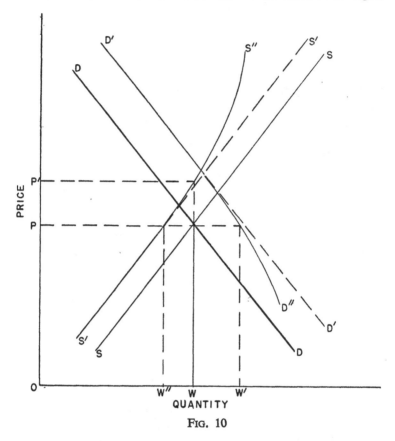

FIG. 10

while a change in the particular goods' price results not in a shift in the curve but in a movement up or down on the curve. The summation of different individual demand schedules gives the industry demand schedule.

It was pointed out in Chapter IV that the ability of an individual to attain the same total satisfaction in the presence of repressed inflation as can be found in a free economy depends upon the shape of the individual's preference curves. An extensive uncontrolled market provides the possibilities of easier and greater substitutability between goods and thereby reduces the convexity of the indifference map. A narrow uncontrolled market produces the reverse. However, as compared with the free market, the presence of any controls reduces the degree of substitutability between goods and lessens the attractiveness of additional money income. As a result each industry's demand curve, generally speaking, will be more inelastic under repressed inflation than it is in a free market. This is portrayed in Fig. 10 by the demand curve $D'D''$. The broken line demand curve $D'D'$ is the shape of the curve in an open inflation.

The above general effects will vary in degree between industries according to the governmental policy with respect to the industry's commodity. In the United Kingdom the usual systems of control of consumption, apart from indirect taxation, were, first, to allocate supplies as between wholesalers and retailers and control the price and, second, to ration the amount which may be purchased by an individual consumer and control the price. In addition to these two alternatives there remains a third—namely, to leave the goods free to obey the laws of supply and demand. We shall consider first the case where the goods are allocated and the prices controlled. In Fig. 10 the original supply and demand schedules of the firm are marked SS and DD respectively. It is assumed that the normal price P, established by the interaction of these two curves, is the price prior to the advent of repressed inflation. The amount demanded at this price is the sum total of all demands made by consumers at that price when their choice is not restricted by controls, and the amount supplied at this price is OW.

It is assumed that under repressed inflation the amount demanded shifts from DD to $D'D''$ and that price control establishes a maximum price of OP, the former equilibrium price, and that the allocation to wholesalers and retailers is based on the quantity OW. If the new demand curve facing the industry is $D'D''$, the unsatisfied demand amounts to WW'. This is the condition of the empty economy in the goods market as described by J. R. Hicks.[1] Prices are not allowed to perform their rationing function, queues form and those first in line receive the goods

[1] J. R. Hicks, 'The Empty Economy', *Lloyds Bank Review*, New Series, No. 5, Lloyds Bank Limited, London, July 1947, pp. 1-15.

while the latecomer is confronted with empty shelves. However, as already pointed out, repressed inflation increases factor costs, and the supply curve will shift to the left—$S'S''$ in Fig. 10. To

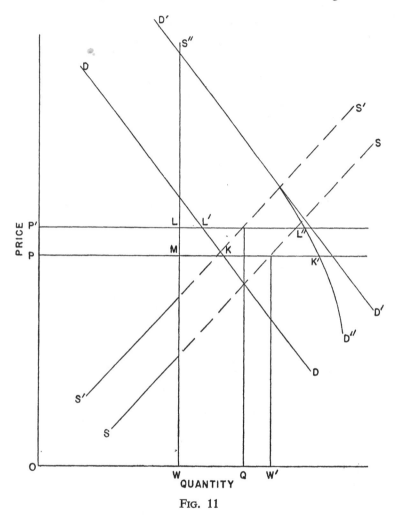

FIG. 11

ensure that production will remain at OW, the controlled price would have to be raised to OP'. Otherwise, the unsatisfied demand will be $W''W'$.

If the controlled price is not adjusted to the new equilibrium level, some producers will be forced out of production. However, it is not in the interests of the government's general policy to have the supply of the goods reduced, and efforts will be made to induce all producers rather than only the most efficient to stay in the industry. Raw materials or factors of production will be allocated to them in a fixed proportion, and the industry may have to be subsidized to cover the higher cost, if a price rise is not considered appropriate.

The United Kingdom experience indicates that the amount allocated was usually much less than sufficient to satisfy the demand at the controlled price, while the price allowed to be charged was usually more than enough to elicit the supply that was allowed to be sold. This is illustrated in Fig. 11. Assume that the government allocates OW to wholesalers and retailers and sets a price OP. At this price the amount which would be supplied in an uncontrolled market given the demand and supply curves SS and DD would be OW'. However, since supply greater than OW will not be forthcoming, the supply curve becomes infinitely inelastic at this point, as is shown by SS''. The unsatisfied demand is MK or MK' at price OP, depending upon the demand curve. Should the supply curve move to the left because of increased costs, the controlled price would likely be raised, for example to OP', and at this price the unsatisfied demand would be LL' or LL''. In the absence of controls the amount freely supplied at this price would be OQ. The establishing of a price greater than that required to call forth the supply OW ensures abnormal profits or rent for all firms, including the marginal firm, who are producing at the time controls are established.

As mentioned above, the second system of consumption control used in the United Kingdom was rationing of the amount which might be obtained by each consumer plus control of the price. The two methods of rationing used were by quantity— e.g. 'four ounces of butter per week'—or by value—'one and sixpence worth a week'—as with meat. The effects of rationing and price control on the shape of the industry's demand curve are illustrated in Table II and Fig. 12.

An industry demand curve is the summation of all individual demand schedules showing the quantities of goods that customers will buy at each possible price. The demand schedule of a consumer is identical with his relative marginal utility schedule. For whatever the goods' price (assuming a perfect market), the quantity which will be consumed is that at which the price is equal to the relative marginal utility. In Table II we assume that

Table II

DEMAND FOR EGGS IN FREE MARKET AND WITH RATION OF 5 EGGS
PER HEA) PER MONTH

Price of eggs (each)	Demand for eggs (No. per month)									
	A		B		C		D		Total	
	Free	Ration	Free	Ration	Free	Ration	Free	Ration	Free	Ration
1s.	1	1	—	—	—	—	—	—	1	1
11d.	1	1	—	—	—	—	—	—	1	1
10d.	1	1	1	1	—	—	—	—	2	2
9d.	2	2	1	1	—	—	—	—	3	3
8d.	3	3	2	2	—	—	—	—	5	5
7d.	4	4	3	3	1	1	—	—	8	8
6d.	6	5	4	4	2	2	—	—	12	11
5d.	8	5	6	5	3	3	—	—	17	13
4d.	10	5	8	5	5	5	—	—	23	15
3d.	13	5	10	5	7	5	1	1	31	16
2d.	17	5	13	5	10	5	2	2	42	17

the goods to be rationed are eggs, and that the ration stipulates that each consumer may have five eggs per month. We assume further that there are only four customers, A, B, C and D, who have different relative marginal utilities at each price.

Assuming there are no controls, then at a price of fivepence A would purchase eight eggs, B six eggs, C three eggs and D none. The total demand for eggs in the free market at this price would be seventeen.

The figures in Table II showing the free market demand for eggs take the form of demand curve DD in Fig. 12. The demand curve becomes DD' when the ration control of five eggs per head per month is imposed. At any government price below seven-pence per egg some consumer will be denied the additional satisfaction he would have received from the purchase of an additional egg. For example, at sixpence per egg A wishes to buy six eggs, but he is denied the purchase of the sixth egg by the ration. At threepence per egg A wishes to purchase thirteen eggs,

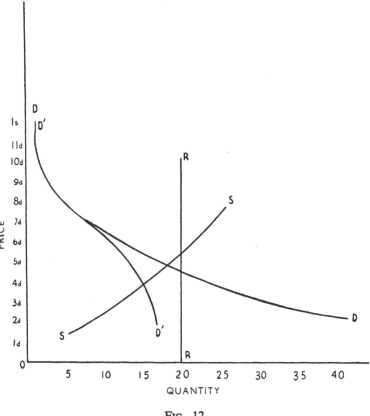

FIG. 12

B wishes to purchase ten eggs and C wishes to buy seven eggs. Only D, who would only buy one egg under any conditions at threepence, is able to receive the same satisfaction in the purchase of eggs in the controlled market as he would have received in a free market. For the rationed demand curve to approach the unrationed curve, customer D and others like him must be allowed to sell their unwanted eggs (in this instance four eggs at a price of threepence) to A, B or C, or the rations must be pooled in some manner.

In Fig. 12, *RR* equals the aggregate maximum of all rations— i.e. twenty eggs. The aggregate amount of eggs purchased will adjust itself to allow for those who do not draw their full ration —e.g. customer D. To prevent the waste of eggs, it would be necessary to fix the price at a level sufficient to bring out this number of eggs only. In the above diagram, since customer D will not draw his ration of five eggs per month at any of the listed prices given in Table II, the total of eggs purchased will be fifteen. Accordingly, the ration price should be set at fourpence per egg. Equilibrium will be attained if at this price producers will furnish the number of eggs required by the ration. If the price is not high enough, subsidies to the producers will be necessary.

If the rationing is done by value instead of by quantity, the effect on the industry's demand curve is the same—i.e. the curve becomes more inelastic. This will happen since the effect of this type of rationing is to allow each individual to purchase only that amount of the rationed goods which the controlled expenditure will command. This type of control is more suitable where there are significant variations as to quality—e.g. meat.

Rationing by quantity and by value have opposite effects upon consumer preferences. Where the ration is by quantity, consumers prefer the better quality goods. Demand for more expensive qualities is stimulated, especially where, as with clothes, they are more durable. Where the rationing is by value, consumers prefer more quantity and less quality. Demand for the cheaper substitute increases, since this is the only way a greater quantity can be obtained for the same amount of money. This was particularly noticeable in the United Kingdom, where the demand for cheaper grades of meats increased as a result of this type of ration.

Although rationing without price control was never practised in the United Kingdom, it is a possible alternative to the types of rationing discussed above.[1] The effect of the ration will be to make the demand curve more inelastic, as in Fig. 12. If there were competition between suppliers, rationing without price

[1] F. W. Paish, 'Open and Repressed Inflation', *The Economic Journal*, Vol. LXIII, No. 251, September 1953, p. 547.

control would not produce high prices. However, the resultant low elasticity of demand would permit large monopoly profits.

The final alternative for the government would be to leave the goods completely uncontrolled. As shown in Fig. 13, price would

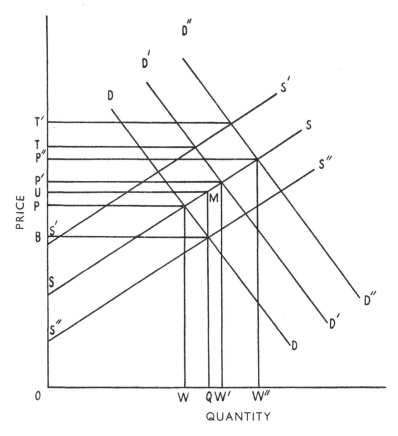

FIG. 13

increase to OP' with a shift in the demand curve to $D'D'$ and the entry of marginal producers who increase the supply to OW', the amount demanded at the higher price. If demand increases to $D''D''$, price rises to OP'' and the amount bought and sold becomes OW''. If the supply curve shifts to the left, because of increased costs, to the position $S'S'$, the price will increase to OT

or OT', and the output bought and sold will be reduced as compared with OW' and OW''. It is assumed that the supply curve $S'S'$ and the demand curves $D'D'$ and $D''D''$ are more inelastic than they would have been in the absence of repressed inflation.

It is very possible that the supply curve of certain industries due to technical reasons may be one of great elasticity over a wide range. If, for example, the uncontrolled goods represent cinemas or bus, plane or train travel, the supply curve will be perfectly horizontal to the X axis at a given price. When all the space available is filled, the supply curve will become perfectly inelastic.

$S''S''$ in Fig. 13 represents the supply curve of an industry which is being subsidized by the government. The effect of the subsidy is that the same or a greater quantity of goods can be supplied to the consumer at a lower price. For example, in our illustration the producer receives a price of OU for his product but the consumer pays only OB and the difference BU is taken care of by the state. The subsidy is merely a negative tax, an amount paid by the government to the producer. Output increases from OW to OQ in our illustration.

CHAPTER VII

The Black Market Pressure against Controls

IN the factor market the pressure against controls can be seen in the struggle by the government to obtain its determined distribution of factor services, in the persistent demands by individual unions for higher wages, in the hoarding of labour by employers and in the reluctance of labour to exchange its effort for discounted savings. The seriousness of the pressure was acknowledged by the British government in their introduction of the Control of Engagements Order, which placed restrictions on labour movements in the agricultural and mining industries.

Besides the pressure of a cost-induced inflation against controls, there is the pressure of the excess demand in the goods market reflected in queues, empty shelves, overcrowded offices, long waiting-lists, oversubscribed order books, voluminous official files, extensive form filling and other general irritations and inefficiencies. These were indirectly reflected in the increased size of the Civil Service. All the effects we have discussed—the appearance of the 'empty economy' in both factor and goods markets where prices are controlled but factors or goods are not rationed; the possibility of monopoly profits as rationing reduces the elasticity of demand for a firm and/or industry's product; the shift of resources into the uncontrolled market which may produce distortions in the economic structure; the unwillingness of labour to offer the same amount of effort for a monetary reward; the search by producers for factors to substitute for labour—all these are a reflection of the tremendous pent-up monetary demand working against the controls of repressed inflation.

In addition, the pressure of controls will probably result in the appearance of a black market. A black market is one in which goods or services are being traded at prices higher than those determined by law. Not infrequently the goods appearing in it are not supposed to be traded at all—e.g. stolen goods. This pressure against controls operates outside the law, and those who seek to trade in black markets run the risk of public prosecution.

A black market appears when the supply of the price controlled and rationed goods is imperfectly controlled by the government. If the government could exercise perfect control over supply, there would be no possibility of any supplies being diverted to a black market and, therefore, no black market.

The degree of attraction which the black market has for sellers and buyers depends among other things upon the severity of the penalties, the type of industry and the effectiveness of the controls over the firm in the industry, the marginal utility of money and the extent of the uncontrolled market. The effectiveness of the controls over the firms and industry depends for the most part on the degree of competition within the industry. In perfect competition, the presence of a large number of sellers and buyers and the ease of entry or egress into or out of an industry and the uniformity of the product as between producers reduces the effectiveness of both controls and penalties. The comparative ease with which buyers and sellers can reach an agreement on prices above the legal limit and keep that agreement from attracting the attention of the legal authorities increases the difficulty of enforcing penalties. The lack of any outward visible form of identification by which the goods can be directly tied to an individual producer increases the difficulty of the authorities in directly identifying and proving an illegal transaction. For example, price control authorities have found black market transactions in agricultural products difficult to detect and prove.

Where the producer practises some form of discrimination and makes the consumer believe his goods to be different from that of his competitor—e.g. by advertising, brand names and product design—the danger of detection of a black market by the authorities is much greater. Consumers are fairly quick to note any rise in prices and the appearance of the goods in the black market. In place of an actual shift of goods away from the legal market toward the black market, the effect of the controls may be to induce production of inferior goods. In imperfect competition it has been found that the industry would supply the legal market with goods of poor quality, saving the better grade of goods for the black market or certain preferred customers.

Other variations of this problem may appear. Given the choice between using labour and raw materials to produce cheaper grade goods for a low price market and quality goods for a higher price market, the producers will prefer that market where the spread between the legal price and their marginal cost is the greatest. For example, the producer may prefer to produce sport shirts instead of ordinary white shirts if the legal price of sport shirts is higher and the production costs are approximately equal. Moreover, many times producers are unable to obtain controlled factors for low priced goods production and cover costs. However, given their available supplies of labour and raw materials, they do find that it is possible to manufacture items for the uncontrolled market where high prices will easily cover costs. The producer feels that it is better to have his plant operating and his labour producing luxury goods than nothing at all. The problem becomes more serious when the producer finds that he is able to obtain his allocated factors and can commence production of controlled goods. Should he stop his production of luxury items and switch the labour employed there to controlled goods production? It is most likely that a strong tendency exists for controlled goods production to be deferred as long as the producer can cash in on the luxury market.

Since unsatisfied demand for controlled goods is the basis upon which a black market exists, the extensiveness of the uncontrolled market becomes an important determinant of the degree of attraction a black market holds for buyers and sellers. An extensive uncontrolled market makes possible greater substitution of the uncontrolled goods for the controlled goods and reduces the convexity of an individual's preference curves. This acts to reduce the extent of unsatisfied demand in the controlled market. Conversely, if the uncontrolled market is very narrow, the danger of goods and factors shifting into the black market is considerably enhanced, and unsatisfied demand is very large.

Under repressed inflation it may be very difficult to extend the area of the uncontrolled market. Aside from imports, the most likely method of extending the area is to decontrol additional goods and services. The success of such a decision depends largely upon the elasticity of the supply of the controlled goods which are to be freed. For reasons already outlined in previous chapters, the supply curve of labour and other factors under repressed inflation will be more inelastic than in an uncontrolled economy. This inelasticity makes it difficult for the government to extend the area of the uncontrolled market, and thereby to reduce the unsatisfied demand, without allowing sharp price increases.

This is illustrated in Fig. 14. Assume at the controlled price

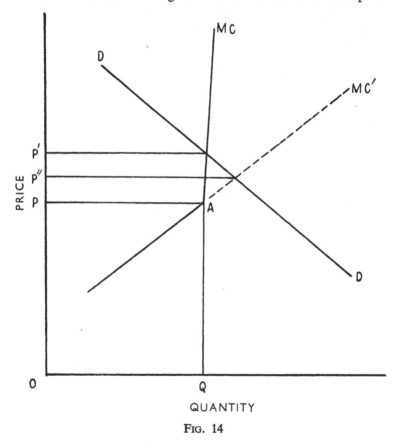

Fig. 14

OP the firm is producing *OQ* with its available labour force and allocated capital, and that this is the optimum output given the firm's factor supply. If any further increase in output beyond *OQ* can only be obtained by additional allocations of capital, the marginal cost curve becomes highly inelastic as more and more capital is combined with a relatively fixed labour supply. The marginal cost curve which would have existed in the absence of repressed inflation becomes a shadow cost curve beyond point A. The increase in price necessary to remove the black market, P', would be greater than the competitive price, P'', would be in the absence of controls. The only recourse open to the government is the imposition of heavier legal penalties and more stringent policing of the controls on economic activity.

The great danger of a black market to an economy is that it promotes additional distortions in the distribution of factors as compared with factor distribution in a free economy and enlarges the chances of the economy's productive structure becoming out of step with government policy. It also restricts the supply of available factors to the controlled industries, enhances their inelasticity and acts to reduce the overall welfare of the economy by attracting factors into less essential production.[1]

---

[1] The theory of the black market has produced considerable discussion. In particular, Professor Boulding has discussed the black market with respect to perfect competition, and Professor Bronfenbrenner with respect to imperfect competition.

Cf. K. E. Boulding, 'A Note on the Theory of the Black Market', *Canadian Journal of Economics and Political Science*, Vol. XIII, February 1947, pp. 115-18; M. Bronfenbrenner, 'Price Control under Imperfect Competition', *American Economic Review*, Vol. 37, No. 1, 1947, pp. 107-120; and Michael Michaely, 'Geometrical Analysis of Black Market Behaviour', *American Economic Review*, Vol. 44, No. 4, 1954, pp. 627-37.

CHAPTER VIII

The Scope of Fiscal Policy

THE adoption of a policy of repressed inflation implies that the government does not believe that the weapons of fiscal and monetary policy alone can cure the body economic without serious injury to the body itself. In particular, governments in the years following World War II did not believe in the use of monetary policy since they considered it purely passive in character. Moreover, the fear of unemployment and the belief that a maintenance of low interest rates is necessary to support investment to prevent unemployment induced many governments to maintain a cheap money policy. Short-run interest rates in the United Kingdom were maintained at a 2 per cent. level for over a decade after the outbreak of World War II. In contrast to the lack of government interest in monetary policy, fiscal policy remained an important weapon to combat inflationary pressures.

The scope of fiscal policy under repressed inflation will be discussed under two headings. The first is concerned with the policy which must be adopted to balance savings with investment demand for factor services in the current period. The second takes into consideration the vast accumulated reserves and wealth of past periods which overhang both the factor and goods markets. In other words, fiscal policy under repressed inflation has to be directed first towards the removal of current inflationary pressures and second toward the removal of latent inflationary pressures arising out of the accumulated savings of previous time periods.

Any country suffering current inflationary pressures under conditions of partial control must recognize first and foremost that unless the current inflationary pressure is contained, the end result can only be economic chaos as the marginal utility of money depreciates more and more. This did happen in Germany after World War II before the currency reforms, and Great Britain was warned of the possibility by Sir Stafford Cripps.

Therefore, we assume that the government in our model economy is determined to provide a budget surplus without extending the size of the uncontrolled market, sufficient in amount —that is, together with business and any personal savings that may arise in the economy—to equal the investment demand for factor services. The current inflationary pressure is to be removed. This is a political step, and the government must have the political courage to follow out the course of action necessitated by such a policy. The government must recognize that a surplus of the size necessary to attain economic stability may likely cause some unemployment of factors. The size of the necessary government surplus may have to be considerable, since, as British experience showed, little is to be expected from the public in the way of increased voluntary savings. If savings are to become a reality, the government must assume prime responsibility.

The great difficulty involved in determining the sufficiency of a budget surplus under an open inflation is the range over which it must operate. Even in a completely free economy infinite substitutability does not exist between factors, and because of the specific nature of some factors it will happen that under an open inflation there will be price increases in some industries while in others there will be only an increased employment of idle resources. In a free market economy the inflationary range covers the area between no price increases and an overall price increase; for example, an inflationary pressure may exist because of the nontransferability of resources before it becomes more easily recognizable in an increase in the general price level.

A budget surplus will impinge directly on prices by removing part of the excess demand in both factor and goods markets. If the surplus is too great, the economy may turn from inflation to deflation. If it is too small, it will have a barely noticeable effect on the price level and the economy. Thus it is a very difficult task to determine the necessary required size of a budget surplus.

In repressed inflation the task becomes even more difficult. Under repressed inflation the inflationary range is expressed in terms of employment. The two extremes are an approximate equality between job opportunities and men to fill them in all industries at one end and more vacancies than men in all industries at the other end. In the controlled market prices can give no indication of what position within this range the economy

F

finds itself placed in at a certain time. A budget surplus impinges directly upon employment under conditions of repressed inflation. Nor can much aid be given by the prices in the uncontrolled market since there exists little comparability between the controlled and uncontrolled prices.

Moreover, in a partially controlled economy where internal stability depends to a great extent on foreign trade, such as Great Britain, the inflationary pressure also appears in the balance of payments, since demand cannot be choked off by rising prices. Under these conditions a government surplus would not only ease the employment demand for labour but it would also tend to restore equilibrium to the balance of payments position.

Once the decision to obtain the necessary budget surplus has been made, the problem becomes a question of method. Between the alternatives of cutting expenditures or raising taxation, which will be the more effective? That method will be effective economically which provides the necessary surplus, and at the same time maintains the greatest possible employment of factors.

If the government attempts to achieve a budget surplus through an increase in taxation, there will follow certain economic effects which will alter both the supply and demand curves in either or both the controlled and the uncontrolled market. Direct taxation affects the factor's willingness to offer its services in exchange for income, and indirect taxation alters the demand curve for the factor's services.

Progressive income taxation has somewhat the same effect on the offer curve of labour as cases 2, 3 and 4 of repressed inflation discussed in Chapter III. It places the individual on a lower indifference curve and therefore induces him to withdraw his labour effort. This is particularly true of high marginal rates of taxation. In addition, progressive income taxation tends to increase the inelasticity of the supply curve of labour, since there is little personal advantage to the individual labourer in offering additional effort for income which not only must be discounted but is also highly taxed. The effect of progressive income taxation on the other factors—e.g. capital—is similar to that of labour, but not to the same degree, since capital—an inanimate object—is more easily subject to direction and control.

An increase in indirect taxation affects the factor market by shifting the demand curve for the factor to the left. The degree to which the demand for labour or any other factor service is affected by indirect taxation will depend upon the elasticity of the demand for the product. An elastic demand will shift the demand curve for labour's services further to the left than an inelastic one.

Indirect taxes are designed on the basis of easy administration from the government's viewpoint and are regressive in character. A regressive indirect tax will to some degree offset the effects of both a progressive income tax and repressed inflation, since its effect is to shift the supply curve of labour to the right. If the tax is placed upon goods with an inelastic demand, the higher prices will induce labour to offer more effort in order to be able to purchase the same amount of goods and services.[1]

In the goods market the effect of increased taxation will first appear in the uncontrolled sector of that market, since there it is possible for the consumer to balance the marginal satisfaction of purchasing the free or uncontrolled item against the marginal satisfaction to be obtained from saving his money. The demand for controlled items, usually the more essential goods, will be reduced only after the marginal satisfaction gained from the purchase of a controlled item is equal to the marginal satisfaction of purchasing an uncontrolled item.

The determinants of a demand pattern for any goods appearing in a free market are liquidity, income, wants and prices of other goods. Broadly speaking, progressive income taxation will affect demand according to its income elasticity; that is, the willingness of a consumer to forgo expenditures on goods as money income decreases. It is a fair assumption that many goods in the uncontrolled sector of the market have a high income elasticity of demand. The demand for controlled items will be reduced only when consumers are so poor relatively that the marginal satisfaction of purchasing goods in the uncontrolled market is equal to the marginal satisfaction of purchasing goods in the controlled market. It may be generally assumed that the income elasticity of demand for controlled goods is very low and

---

[1] A progressive indirect tax would have the same effect on effort as a progressive income tax. It would reduce labour's willingness to offer effort in exchange for a monetary reward. However, a progressive indirect tax is a specially designed piece of tax machinery and not as yet effectively implemented.

purchases will continue to be greater than the supply available, necessitating a maintenance of the controls.

Unfortunately, we cannot assume that the income elasticity of demand of all uncontrolled goods is very high. Consumers acquire new habits, and it is very likely that the income elasticity of demand for some uncontrolled items like tobacco and movies may be very low. The retention of controls over long periods of time strengthens this possibility. Unable to purchase the amount of goods they desired formerly because they are now controlled, consumers may find their tastes changing, and in time the marginal satisfactions gained by purchases of certain uncontrolled goods may increase. If this happens, consumers will strive to maintain the purchase of such goods even with reduced incomes arising out of increased taxation. This was the British experience. The income elasticity of such goods as tobacco, movies and liquor was very low, and attempts to reduce the demand for them by high income taxes as well as high indirect taxes proved relatively ineffective. By contrast, luxury goods had a high income elasticity.

Indirect taxes affect the goods market by distorting price relationships and forcing an alteration in demand patterns. For this reason they are generally considered to be inferior to the income tax, since the income tax leaves the consumer completely free to dispose of his remaining income as he wishes. Moreover, under repressed inflation an indirect tax may not necessarily reduce consumer expenditure because of the presence of large savings already forced on the community by the controls. This possibility is not as important under direct taxation, which decreases personal savings. Inasmuch as these savings are discounted under repressed inflation, the individual will not be too much concerned about paying higher prices because of the taxes. The marginal utility of money to save has decreased so rapidly that higher prices have only a fraction of their former impact on the economy. The individual may as well spend his excess cash in paying higher prices for something he wants as to save it. This possibility has been brought out in Chapter IV, where the effects of repressed inflation on the maximization of an individual's satisfaction were discussed.

If the government decides that heavier direct and indirect taxation is impossible, it may seek to attack the inflationary pressure by using flat-rate taxes—for example, the capital levy and poll tax. The disinflationary effect of a capital levy is extremely doubtful. The destruction of past savings by the government's action is certainly no inducement for consumers to increase their present savings. Confiscation or blocking of money holdings along Russian or Belgian lines would be more effective, but it is out of the question politically until a government's troubles under repressed inflation become spectacular. Neither a poll tax nor an increase in national insurance contributions, both of which are regressive, is politically popular, and even if feasible would be no less provocative of wage demands than taxation of household essentials. To overcome the regressivity of a flat-rate tax, the United Kingdom introduced the 'D' Scheme, which on each item assessed was a flat-rate purchase tax on the excess of the price over a certain figure. The tax was chiefly used for clothing. Cheaper qualities escaped the tax; the better qualities, presumably those with a higher income elasticity, were in effect taxed at a rising average rate.

Another type of direct tax with only a small effect on incentives is the differential rate imposed on distributed profits. However, since dividends are received mainly by those in the higher income groups, an increase in this rate would have no noticeable effect on demand unless the distribution of income approached equality.

We now turn to the suggestion that an increase in the budget surplus be obtained by cutting government expenditures. It must first be recognized that in view of the social philosophy behind repressed inflation the government will be unwilling to cut its welfare expenditure. Other transfer payments may be equally difficult to adjust. Insofar as such cuts are made in expenditure on goods and services, this will release factors directly and does not need to be concerned with the taxpayers' spending habits and preferences, nor with their incentive to work, their efficiency and mobility, and all the delicate issues of money-wage stability. However, a cut in many types of government expenditure will mean no release of suitable resources, since professional workers are mainly involved.

It would seem that a reduction in investment expenditure offers the best possibilities of releasing suitable resources. But where should the cuts be made? Cuts in housing, public works and other building activity are subject to lags and leakages before becoming effective. If the cuts are to be made in capital formation, again the question becomes which cuts will be the most beneficial from an anti-inflationary standpoint and at the same time do the least harm to the productive capacity of the economy. Distinction must be made between productive and unproductive capital. Those capital expenditures are termed productive which will most directly contribute toward greater output and efficiency in the very near future. In economies dependent on foreign trade a further distinction has to be made between those capital expenditures which will contribute toward earning or saving hard currencies—e.g. dollars—and those which will not. Hard currency earning expenditures should have first priority; those which are productive in another sense, second priority; and those which are nonproductive, third priority. The main cuts in capital expenditure should be confined, if possible, to those rating a third priority. This would encompass the field of housing, transport and other items of long-term capital formation. Unfortunately, any cuts of this type are apt to produce considerable resentment on the part of labour, since labour is keenly aware of its relatively privileged position under repressed inflation. Reduction of third priority capital expenditure would not only cause some unemployment, which may become permanent if labour is unwilling to transfer to other industries, but also promote job insecurity, which is particularly disliked by labour, and postpone adequate housing and transportation. Finally, there are political considerations where labour is well organized and votes as a bloc.

The capital expenditure cuts of 1947 in Great Britain are an example of the intricate nature of this problem and of the many social and political considerations which must be taken into account. The cuts were applied where it was administratively simple to handle them. Little attention was given to the overall productivity problem. Any method which merely chops at the demand side of an economic problem without considering the supply function will not accomplish its purpose under repressed inflation. As the following quotation shows, the cuts were the object of severe criticism:

'It is a serious weakness of the White Paper that it hardly contains a positive measure designed to increase productivity by better utilization of existing equipment and of manpower, and that it does not pay sufficient attention to manpower economics outside the field of new construction, to positive measures for facilitating transfers, and to the dangerous tendency of labour hoarding in trade and industry. The Government is right to give priority to stopping the gap in the external balance through foregoing present welfare, but it is running the risk of doing too little about the crux of Britain's short-term economic problem; namely, how to raise a higher output from a given volume of equipment and a given labour force.'[1]

As compared with cuts in government investment expenditures which directly influence employment, cuts in subsidies and social services affect employment through a reduction in demand. Subsidies were costing the British government approximately £450 million a year by 1950. If they had been wiped out, a large saving would have accrued to the British Treasury which could have been used to combat the inflationary pressure. Moreover, subsidies have other economic effects apart from those which follow from the inflationary pressure caused by the heavy government expenditure necessary to finance them. They distort value relationships between commodities and they destroy the efficacy of the comparative costs principle. The consumer pays only a portion of the costs and cannot judge correctly the economic value of the article, and the subsidized price does not represent the true cost of production to the consumer. In addition, they set free excess demand which can be used in the uncontrolled market or used to draw exports into the home market. However, as already pointed out, these economic considerations do not present the complete picture of the subsidy problem. The trade unions would certainly demand and, if necessary, strike for higher wages. If subsidies were cut and taxation also reduced, then labour could not reasonably ask for an increase in wages to compensate for the rise in prices. But reduced taxation means a reduction of the hoped-for budget surplus, and although it would operate to increase the value of money at the margin, it would also increase the inflationary pressure because of the higher marginal propensity to consume

[1] F. A. Burchardt, 'Cuts in Capital Expenditure', *Bulletin of the Oxford University Institute of Statistics*, Vol. 10, No. 1, January 1948, p. 8.

of the lower income groups. The purpose for which a budget surplus was designed would be defeated.

Beside the problem of obtaining the necessary budget surplus to reduce the inflationary pressures, the purpose of a budget surplus under repressed inflation is to free labour and raw materials for employment in those industries believed more vital to the economy and therefore favoured by the government. This raises the question of whether marginal economizing in the uncontrolled goods market will produce the type of factor desired for transfer to the nonconsumption goods industries. It seems reasonable to suppose that those avenues of spending which have been left to the free market absorb resources predominantly of a type not easily transferable elsewhere. For example, one may expect the following uncontrolled goods to be the most affected by decreased consumer demand: entertainment, miscellaneous fancy goods, gadgets, luxury items, travel and holidays. Resources employed in these industries may not be capable of alternative uses. Moreover, even if a significant proportion of transferable resources were released, how many would transfer into vital industries where production is hampered by factor shortages? A greater possibility exists that they would seek employment in higher paying industries while lower paying industries like textiles would remain undermanned. No doubt some would be absorbed by manufacturers already hoarding idle labour in the hope of increased supplies of raw materials. Certainly there is no assurance that under repressed inflation a budget surplus will free the right resources and guarantee their desired distribution as between industries and firms.

By contrast, under an open inflation the impact of a budget surplus is felt throughout the whole economy, not just in a particular section as is the case under a repressed inflation. Prices and profits respond directly to a budget surplus, since the market mechanism is the guiding instrument in the distribution of goods and factors. A budget surplus curtails demand in both factor and goods markets and, with the aid of business and consumer savings, produces a balance between savings and investment which will remove the inflationary pressure. Under repressed inflation, however, the market mechanism cannot perform its necessary function. The economizing that will take place as a result of the disinflationary effect of a budget surplus will be done in the uncontrolled market. Producers of controlled items will find that neither their profits nor their prices will be affected, since prices are below their equilibrium level anyway and relatively insensitive to shifts in demand. The size of a budget surplus required to remove the whole of the excess demand under repressed inflation is probably greater than that required under an open inflation because of the increasing unwillingness of the public to add to its stock of savings. Moreover, the pressure of demand and effects of a budget surplus may be far removed from each other since the excess demand for any controlled item includes demand diverted from other controlled items. Likewise, in the factor market the demand for any controlled factor includes demand diverted from other controlled factors. As a result, the various losses and inefficiencies, the competition for resources, staffing in excess of materials available, the running-down of pipe-line stocks and the appearance of the empty economy may not be mitigated at all by a reduction in government expenditures.

If in addition to the creation of a budget surplus the government decides to extend the area of the free market by withdrawing the controls on many goods, the ability of relative prices to choke off demand and release factor services would be considerably enhanced. However, this method would produce a considerable profit inflation, since the goods formerly controlled are scarce, and excellent opportunities would be provided for the producers to gain quasi-rents. An effort can be made to capture these abnormal profits by increased corporation taxes, an excess profits tax or specially designed indirect taxes. The first two are direct taxes on business profits and would reduce the demand for factor services which may be expected from the producers of goods now not subject to control. However, such taxation would further lower the incentives to efficiency and effort and increase the danger of capital depletion. The indirect tax approach would have the purpose of preventing the abnormal profits from ever accruing in the hands of the producers and force, if possible, their transfer to the government. The goods in the controlled market designed for decontrol would have purchase taxes placed on them, which would be increased if prices of the items rose over a certain agreed-upon level.

The extension of the free market and higher prices would

increase relatively the marginal utility of money to save and labour's willingness to exchange effort for money. There is also a greater likelihood of factors being released which may be transferred into other production. If the government is to avoid marginal economizing taking place in the uncontrolled market only, some discriminatory fiscal approach is needed whereby the market mechanism can be harnessed to the cause of economic stability.

However, the difficulties of such a proposal must be recognized. Besides the colossal administrative difficulties in planning, the almost certain threat of a wage-price spiral exists since prices will increase. As explained in Chapter II, the policy of any government under repressed inflation must be based on stability of prices and wages; otherwise it will be impossible for the controls to maintain the government's desired distribution of factor services between favoured and nonfavoured industries and prevent inflation. Should this danger eventuate, the good effects of the disinflationary budget surplus would be nullified. Moreover, if taxes are already at a high level and have had noticeably adverse effects on labour effort and business efficiency, as they had in Great Britain, any further increase would make the burden unbearable.

As pointed out at the beginning of this chapter, it is necessary in discussing the scope of fiscal policy to consider the vast accumulated reserves and wealth of past periods. In an open inflation the accumulated savings are being depreciated in real value terms by rising prices, while in a repressed inflation savings retain more of their real value and do not have to be written off so quickly. Therefore, in a post-war period the economy is faced with a greater volume of real savings than would otherwise have been the case. Though it does not guarantee that prices will not increase, repressed inflation does succeed in postponing the rise.

The latent wealth and excess reserves of past periods are a constant threat to the success of the government's efforts to remove inflationary pressures. Broadly speaking, the government has three alternatives in attempting to remove this threat: (1) it can remove all controls and allow an open inflation; (2) it can seek to reduce or destroy the private wealth and excess liquidity; or (3) it can seek to so increase productivity that goods and services at the controlled prices will satisfy the excess demand. When supply and demand equate at the controlled prices, the controls would be removed. Thus the government could hope to work off the inflation.

No further attention need be paid to the first alternative because of political and social considerations. Real income would shift from labour to profits, and most assuredly the economy would erupt in a series of strikes, added to which the end result of such a policy may well be destruction of the price mechanism.

With regard to destroying the latent inflation, political as well as economic circumstances must be considered. As mentioned previously in this chapter, the blocking of past accumulated savings in a manner similar to that adopted by Belgium requires that any government face a spectacular political situation necessitating such a solution and that the solution be acceptable to the people. Unless this happens, a capital levy or a forced loan would cause the public to distrust the country's currency even more. This distrust would immediately act to lessen labour effort and further decrease the marginal utility of savings. Furthermore, the magnitude of such a step must be recognized. If repressed inflation has existed over many years, the accumulated past savings and wealth will be enormous. To wipe this out with one capital levy is impossible unless the government is willing to risk everything to restore the free market economy. It is very likely that such action would destroy rather than aid the economy, because of the loss of confidence in the currency and the fear that savings are worthless. Added to which, the government has made explicit promises in encouraging the people to save during the war years concerning the good things in life that they could purchase in a return to peace. To destroy such savings may act to effectively destroy any trust the people may have in their government.

We are left, therefore, with the third alternative. The government endeavours to increase productivity and by the maintenance of a high level of output in the economy it hopes that the inflationary pressure of accumulated savings and wealth will gradually work itself off over the years. This is the only solution possible politically. There is the further point that repressed inflation is conducive to a cost-induced inflation which pushes prices higher and higher. The price rise acts to destroy part of the inflationary pressure of past savings as their real value depreciates. Thus the government attacks the pressure from two sides. It activates the inflation by allowing prices to be pushed up to some extent, pointing out to the people that because of their country's economic position they must accept a lowering of consumption standards for the nation's welfare, and it strives to increase output which will in time release more goods for home consumption. This was the policy adopted by the British government, and by mid-1950 most of this inflationary pressure had disappeared or had been rendered inactive: 'The evidence seems to show that by the middle of 1950 steady adherence to the policy of disinflation had brought about a fairly satisfactory balance between total demand and total supply. Demand continued to run at a high level, but not so high a level as to cause any marked symptoms of inflation. The level of unemployment remained extremely low. The continued rise of consumer prices during the year was due to the rise in import prices rather than to any inflation of internal costs. There was a general tendency for demand to become more competitive, and increased supplies made it possible for many price controls to be suspended by the middle of the year. There was a general rise in retail stocks.'[1]

The whole problem of fiscal policy is not entirely an economic one. It is, perhaps primarily, a social and political one. Cuts in national expenditures to reduce the current inflationary pressure, which would meet the two criteria mentioned, require harsh decisions on the government's part. Cuts in housing, public and long-term capital expenditures could release resources for transfer to export production and create a budget surplus which would produce internal stability. But unemployment could increase, since labour would be left with the alternatives of accepting work in exporting industries or going on the dole, and it depends on labour which alternative will be accepted. It is doubtful if any government with a strong and politically active labour force, as was the case in Great Britain, could long retain its political popularity if subsidy and social service expenditures were cut, or their taxes increased. From the government's point of view it is politically more astute to announce small and perhaps meaningless reductions in capital expenditure rather than to adopt a policy which carries with it heavy political repercussions. Economic analysis suggests that such cuts must be of a

[1] *Economic Survey for 1951* (Cmd. 8195), p. 40.

sizeable magnitude to be effective, and here again the government is faced with a political problem.

Similarly, any action directly to eliminate the danger of the inflationary pressure of past accumulated savings and wealth is fraught with political danger.

CHAPTER IX

Considerations and Conclusions

An inflationary pressure arises in an economy whenever the planned expenditures on factor services by nonconsumption producers are greater than the planned voluntary release of factors through savings. Voluntary savings may be taken as a measure of the number of factors the economy willingly gives up for employment in the nonconsumption industries. Whether the inflationary pressure will result in price increases depends primarily upon the availability of factor services in the factor market. If there is unemployed labour and complementary factors are available in the right proportion, the inflationary pressure will lead to greater output and income and there will be no price inflation. However, if there are no unemployed factors, prices will rise to force sufficient savings out of the economy and thereby release the factors to satisfy the investment demand for factor services. In a condition of full employment, wherever savings are less than the investment expenditures on factor services, the distribution of factors between investment and consumption industries is not in accordance with consumer desires. Where prices alone act as the rationing agent for factors and goods in the respective markets, we have an open inflation. But if a government is determined to maintain a given proportion of factors in the investment industries which is greater than the willing release of factors through voluntary savings and, at the same time, prevent price increases in both markets, the surest method of increasing savings is the imposition of arbitrary controls in the factor and goods markets. Where the government takes this action, the nature of the inflation changes from that of an open to a repressed inflation. The controls are arbitrary in the sense that they operate outside of and not through the price system. Their purpose is the repression of price increases and the results that follow therefrom.

Whether repression is successful or not depends primarily upon the willingness of the public to accept the greatly increased savings forced on them by the controls. During a war the powerful emotional factor of patriotism acts to assure compliance with the controls. But in peace-time this emotional element no longer exists, and the public, with its vast hoard of liquid savings, acquired because of repression during the war years, will increase sharply its consumption expenditures in the goods market. Likewise the large liquid reserves of businessmen and producers enable them to increase heavily their demand for factor services. Thus, if a government is to avoid competitive bidding for factors and prevent inflation in the goods market, it must continue the controls in both the factor and goods markets.

A country which has suffered severe destruction during the war, as so many of the European countries did, has virtually little choice in the adoption of a policy of repressed inflation. Besides the economic considerations, there are powerful social and political forces which are of major importance. It is an age of increased social consciousness as reflected in the spread of social legislation throughout the world. No longer can a government coldly adopt a policy which would cause hardship to the lower income groups. And unless a country has a tremendous productive capacity which can be rapidly mobilized, an open inflation would lead to just that. It is understandable why after a war governments are loath to accept the economic decisions of a market mechanism. With the tremendous demand for both factors and goods, the market mechanism would ration strictly according to ability to pay. This would mean tremendous wage and factor price increases which in turn increase production costs in the factor market and shift real income from labour to profits in the goods market. Unquestionably the economy would erupt in a series of strikes as labour sought to prevent its loss of real income. After the inflationary pressure had spent itself, the economy could enter upon a ruinous deflation, which would result in heavy unemployment. Thus, to prevent cost increases, shifts in real income away from labour, possible deflation and unemployment, and, at the same time, accomplish its tremendous investment programme, governments attempt to repress the operations of the market mechanism and substitute a system of controls. The market mechanism through prices still continues partially to perform its cost, income and rationing functions. However, it has been denied its position of primacy.

An investigation of repressed inflation is, therefore, mainly an investigation of the operation of controls on the economy to determine how successfully they equate savings with investment demand for factor services without price increases. As pointed out in Chapter III, it is possible to identify four degrees or cases of repressed inflation classified according to the extent of the controls.[1] This study has concerned itself mainly with case 4, since it is typical of the democratic countries trying to control inflationary pressures and recover from the devastation of the war. The first three cases would only be workable in countries without a democratic government. Therefore, for the purposes of this study, repressed inflation has been defined as the partial control of essential goods and factors, the controls having been carried to the extent politically possible in a democratic country. The study concentrates on the operation and effects of the controls imposed to stem the excess demand in both markets and force sufficient savings in the economy to balance the heavy investment demand for factors. It must be understood that under repressed inflation there are two types of controls: those that act to restrain consumer demand and prevent price increases, and those that allocate factor services and distribute them in accordance with a planned investment programme. Thus controls have two purposes:

1. To force sufficient personal savings out of the economy in the goods market which together with other savings (business

---

[1] Case 1 is where all goods and factors are completely controlled. The economy is under complete repression, so that income over and above the amount necessary to purchase the rationed goods and factors is relatively useless. Savings have little attraction, therefore, for the general public. In case 2, the government promises that savings will have some value sometime in the future. Money income over and above the amount necessary to purchase the rationed goods acquires some meaning, that is, the marginal utility of money to save increases. In case 3, the economic significance of money to save increases still further if the government promises that all savings will have full value at a given future date. Case 4 takes the form of a partially controlled inflation. Only essential consumer items in short supply are controlled in the goods market, and in the factor market the factors land and capital are most liable to be allocated through building licences and raw materials allocation.

and government) will balance investment demand for factor services.

2. To provide the means in the factor market whereby the economy can carry out its planned investment programme.

Therefore, we can measure the effectiveness of repressed inflation by the degree to which (1) general price increases are prevented in the economy, and (2) the government's target of planned investment is accomplished.

To restrain excess consumer demand from preventing the mobilization of resources in the government-favoured industries, chief reliance is placed on controls of supplies or purchases of essential commodities through rationing and price control in the goods market and the use of manufacturing licences, etc., to allocate scarce factors in the factor market. In Great Britain such licences were issued through the Board of Trade. In addition, although price control limited monopoly profits, the controlled prices were in practice always fixed on a 'cost-plus' basis which assured high profits for even the less efficient producer.

Besides such direct controls, the government attempts to curtail the amount of disposable income by imposing direct and indirect taxes, by encouraging wage restraint on the part of the trade unions with its policy of price stability, by differential taxes on distributed and undistributed profits and by encouraging the willingness of businessmen to follow government policy and restrain dividend distribution.

Fundamental to the success of the government's entire policy is the effect of the controls on the valuation of marginal savings, as was pointed out in Chapter III. If marginal savings are viewed favourably, additional labour effort will be offered. Greater supplies will be forthcoming as labour is combined with other factors in optimum proportions, and the pressure of excess demand will be reduced. Whether marginal savings are viewed favourably depends greatly on the consumer's ability to achieve satisfaction in the disposal of his income in the controlled and uncontrolled markets, as was discussed in Chapter IV. The other general effects of repressed inflation influence the allocation of factor services and the market conditions facing the firm and industry.

Unfortunately, repressed inflation is extremely conducive to a

G

wage-cost inflation. This is one of the most serious of all the effects of repressed inflation. The controls and the excess demand combine in several ways to bring about a loss in productivity which lowers the consumer's real income and is the initial cause of such an inflation. The loss of productivity arises from many different sources, all primarily the result of the government's policy of repression. These may be listed as follows:

1. The increasing reluctance of labour to offer effort in exchange for savings, which reduces labour's productivity and increases rigidities in the economy.

2. The declining productivity of the substitute factors as greater dosages are applied to a fixed supply of labour beyond the optimum factor combination point.

3. The appearance of bottlenecks because of capital shortages.

4. The hoarding of labour by producers in anticipation of greater capital or raw material allocations by the government.

5. The presence of easy profits which promotes irresponsibility on the part of management toward economies of production.

6. The continuation of the high cost marginal producer in production because of the controls which form an umbrella of protection under which he can continue to operate.

7. The possibility that highly progressive marginal rates of income taxation imposed to combat the inflation may reduce the amount of labour effort offered.

All of the above appear under repressed inflation, and all tend to reduce the productivity of the economy, thereby increasing the pressure against controls.

Thus it may be concluded that under repressed inflation it is not likely that a stable price level can be maintained. Costs are always tending to push prices up. Repressed inflation is unlikely to stabilize the general level of prices; it can only control the rate at which prices are rising.

Besides the danger of wage-cost inflation, there are other effects of repressed inflation which may be described conveniently by tracing through the results discernible in the goods and factor markets respectively. It must be recognized, however, that it is impossible to separate with complete clarity the effects of the inflation from the effects of the controls. Repressed inflation is, by definition, a composite of the two.

For convenience, the effects of repressed inflation are divided under the following subheadings:

1. The results of the excess demand in the factor and goods markets.

2. The results of controls in the factor and goods markets.

3. The problem of consumer satisfaction.

4. The problem of investment and capital.

THE RESULTS OF EXCESS DEMAND

Repressed inflation does not remove any of the problems of an excess demand situation. For example, a wage-price spiral may be held in check by heavy subsidy expenditures on the part of the government and yet be ready to break out the moment subsidies are not increased or maintained.[1] It becomes almost impossible for governments in peace-time successfully to curtail budget expenditures for such items as food, low-cost housing, etc. The moment expenditures are reduced and labour feels its loss of real income sharply, the trade unions are forced to demand wage increases and the vicious wage-price spiral commences.

The excess demand sharply reduces factor mobility. The inflationary pressure of excess demand may be recognized in the inability of the government to accomplish its target of manpower distribution between industries within the economy. The hoarding of labour on the part of firms in anticipation of easier and larger capital or raw materials allocations is made possible by the easy profits which exist under repressed inflation. The expansion of many service industries fostered by the excess demand spilling over from the controlled market into the free market increases the demand for factor services. The extent of the excess

---

[1] Subsidies are usually necessary under repressed inflation to reduce the danger of a wage-price spiral. Yet subsidies cannot hold the line in the face of increasing costs on imported supplies. Successful application is most likely in the case of home-produced agricultural produce. Cf. J. J. Polak, 'On the Theory of Price Control', *The Review of Economic Statistics*, Vol. 27, February 1945, pp. 10-16.

demand in Great Britain could be measured by the figure for unemployment. For example, in 1950 unemployment was something less than 2 per cent. of the total labour force. At such a level jobs chased workers and there existed little incentive for labour to seek out work opportunities.

The appearance of the 'empty economy' is another factor directly attributable to the workings of excess demand. Where items are price controlled but no effective attempt is made to force demand and supply to balance at some agreed price, resources will be drawn off too fast from the industrial pipeline into final output and final consumption, with a consequent threat to the continuity and efficiency of production and distribution. The coal crisis in the winter of 1946-47 in Great Britain may be attributed in part to the absence of effective measures to balance demand with supply at the controlled price. Coal rationing became effective after the crisis had developed.

Should an economy depend upon foreign trade, to a large extent importing necessary foodstuffs and raw materials and exporting finished products, the presence of excess demand presents another grave problem. Total expenditures on factor services is made up of domestic expenditures plus exports. As domestic expenditures go up, the national money income increases, and likewise imports will rise, since the marginal propensity to import is a function of the amount of domestic expenditure. The increased expenditure on imports creates a drain on foreign exchange reserves, and in countries such as Great Britain, where the balance of payments occupies a central position in the economic picture, immediate steps must be taken to check the loss of foreign exchange reserves such as import quotas and exchange restrictions. If a country under repressed inflation has sufficiently large reserves to withstand heavy withdrawals, the chance that repressed inflation will be able to fulfil its assigned rôle will be greatly enhanced. The inflow of large quantities of foreign goods would reduce the inflationary pressure, allow the price level to be more easily stabilized, enhance the value of money in the eyes of the factors of production and thus induce a greater willingness to exchange effort for money payments. Also producers would be able to obtain capital and raw materials and an easier and smoother flow in production would follow. The tendency for rising costs of production would be greatly reduced, and correspondingly the danger of a wage-cost inflation.

However, where the economy lacks extensive foreign exchange reserves, the effects of the controls will endanger the exchange reserves. Because of the inability to purchase imports, consumption of goods destined for export markets may occur, drawing down sharply the foreign exchange earnings of the economy and thereby endangering the balance of payments. This threat to the successful attainment of the export target requires additional controls to ensure that those goods produced for export are actually entering the export market. The loss of exports to the home market contributed to the different payments crises suffered by Great Britain for several years following World War II.

It is unlikely, however, that the producers of the export goods will see the payments problem in the same light as the government. The presence of easy profits and the heavier risks of foreign markets will influence the producers to increase their sales in the home market. It is remarkable how at the end of successive accounting periods in Great Britain it has been discovered that more goods designed for export have been drawn into home consumption than was planned. Thus the presence of excess demand forces controls over imports and exports and makes repressed inflation incompatible with a system of free trade.[1]

In any case there is apt to be a conflict between investment and export targets, particularly in an economy suffering from the ravages of war and capital depletion of plant and equipment. The demand for capital resources, labour and raw materials for an extensive export programme, and the demand for home investment in housing, plant and equipment, road construction, etc., cannot both be satisfied. The failure of the export target in Great Britain may be attributed to a large extent to the increasing volume of home investment. The government's attempt to maintain its export target in the face of heavy home investment demand by further restrictions on home consumption led to rising dissatisfaction in the ranks of labour and other factors. But the problem in the export industries is primarily one of

[1] Bertil Ohlin, *The Problem of Employment Stabilization*, New York, Columbia University Press, 1949, p. 25.

production, not of consumption. Bottlenecks which arise under repressed inflation because of allocation necessitated by the excess demand for factors are the main obstacles to the attainment of the export target.

THE RESULTS OF CONTROLS IN THE FACTOR AND GOODS MARKET

Under repressed inflation money is overshadowed by coupons and shopping opportunities. Whether the purchase of substitute goods will give the consumer the sum total of satisfaction he desires becomes the crucial issue. If it does, the marginal utility of money income will be maintained; if it does not, then at what point will labour refuse to accept savings in exchange for the same or additional effort? In a war economy this critical point may never be reached because of the emotional feelings aroused by patriotic appeals which make labour willingly accept savings in exchange for additional effort. Unfortunately, such emotions are not present in peace-time. The public after the restraints suffered during the war now wants to rid itself of those restraints and taste the fruits of victory. Money is no object in the purchase of a long-denied but desired good. In a spending spree designed to forget the dark days of war and recapture quickly the joys of peace, so effectively described by many politicians, the public literally throws away its money.

It is to prevent the open inflation which would result from such an understandable reaction on the part of the public that governments believe controls are necessary and must be continued. The controls also aid the government to re-equip industry, increase social investment and expand exports to recapture foreign markets and thereby help restore the pre-war standard of living. However, to assure the success of the tremendous investment expansion which must be undertaken, controls alone are not enough. Successful accomplishments depend on the ready acceptance by the public of further restraints, which, in economic terms, means the willing exchange of factor services for increasing amounts of savings.

Though there is less chance under a partially controlled inflation that the critical point will be reached, a certain condition must be fulfilled—namely, the public must believe in the constancy of the value of the economy's currency. The fulfilment of this condition turns on (1) the willingness of the factors to accept substitute goods, (2) the presence of a plentiful supply of such goods, and (3) a belief that the government's action is the only possible solution and that the solution is in the hands of just and capable men. If money has value and thrift is honoured by the community, savings are viewed with respect by the factors. Successful results will follow from the government's policy, since the factors will obey the law of equal monetary advantage. Labour effort will not be withheld from the market, and the producer will be able to obtain the necessary labour force and so reach his optimum output. The law of comparative costs will operate because specialization in the cheap cost factor is possible.

A study of the British economy from 1945 to 1949 does not illustrate this best of all possible worlds with respect to repressed inflation. Perhaps the greatest contribution to the success of repressed inflation in Great Britain was the character of the British worker and businessman, as shown by their willing response to patriotic appeals for increased production and restraints on normal business practices. That this is not characteristic of the whole British working population may be granted. But, by and large, the British worker, the trade unions and the businessmen are to be highly congratulated on their willingness to listen and to accept the appeals made to them by the government. However, even in this favourable atmosphere, the British economy approached the degenerative stages of repressed inflation. Absenteeism in the mines, the difficulty in getting labour to shift to those industries where it was most urgently needed, the shift of labour to industries frowned upon by the government, the appearance of bottlenecks in production because of the inability to obtain capital goods, materials or labour, and the high and rigid costs of the British economy all illustrate the less favourable side of repressed inflation. The shift of labour from the coal-mines had taken place in spite of high wages paid to the miners and the patriotic appeals by the British government. Inasmuch as under repressed inflation high wages mean little more than larger amounts of savings, nonmonetary advantages, like living in a large city with its many amenities or the chance to work at a position higher on the social scale, assume greater importance. It may be said that under repressed inflation labour is inelastic with respect to money but elastic with respect to nonmonetary advantages.

It has been pointed out in Chapter II that the nature of repressed inflation is such that some type of control over labour must be maintained. The most likely form it will take in a democratic country is that practised by Great Britain, where the government policy of wage and price stabilization achieved a measure of control over wages. Since prices are constantly subject to upward revision because of the susceptibility of the economy under repressed inflation to a cost-induced inflation, it is natural, therefore, to expect pressure from the trade unions for higher wages.

Peculiarly enough, while repressed inflation means low labour mobility between industries, there exists a high labour turnover between firms. There is a meaningless movement of workers from one firm to another, which reduces the firms' efficiency of production and operation. This is understandable since repressed inflation tends to maintain the inefficient firm in production either through subsidization or controls on prices and factors which assure profits by keeping costs down. The ability of the marginal firm to stay in production is one of the reasons for the presence of a cost-induced inflation and further testifies to the relegation of the law of comparative costs to the economic ashcan.

As described in Chapter V, controls in the factor market are essential if the government's investment policy is to be successful. However, such controls are arbitrary and may easily dictate an allocation of factors out of step with economic reality.

THE PROBLEM OF CONSUMER SATISFACTION

The problem of consumer satisfaction cannot be placed under either of the two previous headings since it vitally concerns both at the same time. Care must be taken to understand the worker's demand for higher wages. If money has value in the eyes of labour, repressed inflation will not produce a lessening in labour effort. However, it is equally possible to argue that the demand for higher wages arises out of labour's belief that it has a right to the higher wages. Why must a labourer offer greater effort to obtain a position which by right he should have? If labour has this attitude, increased wages will not induce greater effort since they are awards for a standard of living which has become a right in labour's eyes. In this case labour assumes that the un-rationed goods are included within the definition of a standard of living, and if the prices of such goods rise, as is likely, labour will consider that it has suffered a loss in its living standard. Some of Britain's persistent wage-cost problems in the years following World War II can be analysed from this viewpoint.

If repressed inflation is continued over many years, the sense of frustration either deepens or consumer preferences and tastes may change in favour of the substitute goods. If the frustration deepens, then the satisfaction gained from substitute goods may decline and the memories of former days with plenty of meat become more nostalgic. If tastes change, satisfaction may increase. Which attitude will be predominant cannot be known.

Since the ability of the factors acting as consumers to obtain a sum total of satisfactions is of the greatest importance under repressed inflation, their number of visits to the cinema, the days spent on vacation or the hours spent in travel should not call forth bitter pronouncements by government leaders and others. Without these satisfactions the level of production and the willingness of labour to offer more effort would decline. The presence of an adequate supply of such substitute goods is a bulwark against the threatening critical point of repressed inflation.

Thus there exist two sides to the problem of dissaving under repressed inflation. Dissaving increases the inflationary pressure in the economy, but on the other hand it also allows labour to achieve a degree of satisfaction not otherwise possible. It is mis-leading to discuss the dangers of a repressed inflation without recognising that there may be important offsetting considera-tions on the credit side of the ledger.

The whole problem of consumer satisfaction under repressed inflation sheds considerable light on the government's invest-ment policy in peace-time. Allocation of investment resources on a priority basis to the construction of houses and similar schemes can be partially explained in this way. The tremendous destruction caused by the war in Great Britain, plus an increase in the population and marriages, demanded that housing be increased as rapidly as possible. It is to be taken for granted that housing shortages cause great social unrest and increase the immobility of labour. As housing becomes more abundant at low subsidized rents, labour's sum total of satisfactions is increased. Whenever housing or like investment is condemned as demanding too much of the total available resources in the economy, the point must be remembered that an increase in labour's satisfaction will increase the willingness of labour to offer more effort and thus operate to lessen the danger of approaching the critical point.

Unfortunately, this is not the whole investment picture. Investment guided by principles of government priority and allocation runs the excellent chance of producing maladjustment of resources in the favoured industries. This possibility was discussed in Chapter V. In addition, there are two other weighty considerations to be borne in mind. The allocation of investment resources on a social priority basis lessens the amount of total resources available to expand necessary production. Will the satisfactions received by the lower income groups counterbalance the rising costs and lessened production in export and other industries? If war's destruction of plant and equipment and the heavy loss of foreign investments reduced the ability of an island economy like Great Britain to sustain an acceptable standard of living, was the gain of satisfaction through investment in long-run social priorities too high a price to pay? Perhaps it would be better to run the risk of greater labour unrest and immobility by cutting investment in such industries as housing and concentrating on the production of exports. There is no question that a government's demand for resources will seriously limit the ability of many producers to obtain the amounts necessary to continue the volume of production desired. If the demand is reduced, allocations may prove unnecessary. Re-equipment of depreciated industries would speed up and production of goods for both the internal and the external markets would increase; costs would tend to fall. New productive techniques may be introduced, if the capital is available, and thus the productivity of the factor capital increases. There seems little question that repressed inflation may operate to lessen economic progress, particularly if capital is rationed.

In terms of consumer satisfaction, it can be argued that increased investment in plant and machinery may allow a greater allocation to the home market because of increased production, or the importation of foreign goods because of increased exports. This satisfaction may or may not counterbalance the loss of the satisfaction obtainable from a programme of long-term social priority investment such as low-cost housing.

THE PROBLEM OF INVESTMENT AND CAPITAL

It is not surprising to find under repressed inflation a condition of overinvestment developing. By overinvestment in this context we mean a desire by producers to make investment decisions and commit factors to investment production in amounts greater than the government's planned programme. Since profits in both controlled and uncontrolled items are great, additional investment is strongly desired.

To curb this desire, material allocation, production control and building licences may be used to restrict investment demand. In addition, a government agency, such as the Capital Issues Committee in Great Britain, may be set up to control the issue of any new stock or debenture and thereby prevent any new company or existing concern from making additional claims on factor resources. The government may also adopt a policy of encouraging large business savings by the adoption of a tax on distributed profits. In Great Britain in 1950 business and government savings accounted for over 95 per cent. of the total saving done in the economy.

The effect of this on the economy is that investment decisions are concentrated almost entirely in the hands of government ministers or existing businesses. The presence of risk capital available for investment purposes to any individual or company outside of this range is virtually nil. The public does not have the savings to give to untried investment, and certainly neither the government nor business will be apt to risk funds anywhere but in their own preconceived investment programmes. Thus the initiative of the individual without capital of his own is severely limited. The complete restriction of investment decisions to the government and established businesses does not augur well for the fostering of competitive industry. In fact, the complete drying up of risk capital in an economy could result in the universal control of the economy by monopolies and cartels in the hands of the government and private business.

Even though private business is forced to save a great deal through the controls imposed by the government, there still exists the threat of capital depletion under repressed inflation. The most usual basis on which controlled prices are fixed is cost plus a normal profit. This cost plus normal profit basis may not . be sufficient to cover depreciation and depletion of capital assets. Unless the repression is complete and universal, capital and replacement costs increase markedly, and even with high profits it is very likely that businesses will not retain enough earnings to cover the rising replacement costs. If the government allows greater depreciation allowances, it lays itself open to the charge by trade unions that private business is earning and re-taining too great a profit. This charge was made in Great Britain and was the basis of increased wage demands by unions who claimed that the higher wages could be paid out of profits and the accumulated surpluses of business concerns.

In final consideration of the effects of repressed inflation, it must not be forgotten that any economic policy has its good as well as its bad effects. The bad effects of repressed inflation have been pointed out and perhaps over-emphasized. Full value must be given to the advantages which repressed inflation can bring to a nation. These may be summarized as follows:

1. Repressed inflation acts strongly to prevent the shift in real income from the lower income groups to the higher income groups, and prevents, therefore, the redistribution of wealth in favour of the higher income groups which happens under an open inflation.

An open inflation has several safety valves which operate to mitigate against the continuation of the inflation. The transfer of income from wages to profits produces greater savings, since the propensity to save of the higher income groups is greater than that of the lower income groups. Rising prices restrict consumer demand and equate this demand with supply. Increasing interest rates curb investment expenditure on factor services. Unless the inflation adopts the character of a hyper-inflation, the operation of the price mechanism will bring a halt to excessive expenditure.

Repressed inflation refuses to allow this to happen. Consumer demand is not restricted by rising prices. There is not the shift of income from wages to profit with its salutary effect of greater savings, since repressed inflation maintains to a great extent the real income of the lower income groups. Nor are rising interest rates allowed to restrict the investment demand for factor services.

The continuing maintenance of a relatively stable level of real income for the lower income groups is one of the salient features of repressed inflation. To restrict the inflationary pressure without resorting to additional controls and extension of the area of repression, the government must rely upon taxation to: (1) dampen expenditures on factors in the factor market, and (2) curtail the disposal of factor income in the goods market. This means heavy marginal income taxation with its effects on labour effort, price distortions because of the higher indirect taxes, which may produce a cost inflation, and the possibility of producing unemployment. However, to many people, the prevention of the shift in real income away from labour is of such social importance as to outweigh the danger of any such possibilities.

2. The real standard of living of the lower income groups is not only protected under repressed inflation but very often increased. Repressed inflation can operate to shift wealth from the upper income groups to the lower income groups, mainly through specially fostered social services and rations which ensure a definite and fair share of scarce supplies.

3. Repressed inflation allows the government to force through an investment programme very likely greater than that possible in the absence of repressed inflation and in the presence of an open inflation.

4. Repressed inflation should stimulate investment and capital formation in low-cost mass producing industries, and increase productivity by the use of more capital equipment. A vast market is created by repressed inflation for the low-cost producer. This could mean a great revolution in industrial production if the emphasis shifts from quality to quantity production.

5. It is comparatively easy to prevent the appearance of a depression and unemployment by merely releasing some of the controls and allowing the forced savings to express themselves in a widening free market.

6. The scarcity of labour under repressed inflation promotes the use of substitute factors and therefore induces producers to

seek new methods for increasing production. Furthermore, this vast increase in capital formation is not so bitterly opposed by labour, since the fear of unemployment is kept at a minimum.

How any government will evaluate these advantages and disadvantages depends upon the social and economic conditions facing it. If such conditions are similar to those which faced Great Britain in 1945, the price of repressed inflation is cheaper than the price of open inflation. An open inflation would produce as great distortions as a repressed inflation and enhance the danger of unemployment and social unrest both during and after the inflation. Also the danger that the British economy might reach the critical point in repressed inflation was lessened by the historical stability of the British pound. Any government fortunate enough to have a currency world-renowned for its stability can adopt a policy of repressed inflation with an easier conscience, for this fact will enhance the value of money to save. In Germany the history of the previous German inflation weakened the hope of the government in its policy of repression. Again the loyalty to and willing acceptance of the British government and its policies by the people, and particularly by labour, was a potent force in reducing the dangers of repressed inflation.

The main political and social consideration in Great Britain behind the adoption of the policy of repressed inflation was the fear of unemployment on the part of labour inherited from the past and their determination to prevent wealth and income from determining the distribution of scarce consumer goods. The concept of fair shares and full employment is prominent in Labour Party philosophy. In fact, there is the suggestion that the intellectuals of the Labour Party believe controls are a good thing and should be made permanent. Thus, whatever policy is adopted will also depend somewhat upon the political and social philosophy of the government in power.

CHAPTER X

Postscript: 1950-1954

UNFORTUNATELY for the United Kingdom, 1950 did not mean the end of all inflationary pressures. New pressures soon arose, some from causes similar to those which existed in 1945 and others from completely different sources. In contrast to a policy of repressed inflation, chief reliance was placed on fiscal and monetary policy to stem the new inflationary pressures.

The departure from the policy of repressed inflation and the adoption of older, more classical methods of restoring economic equilibrium necessitate a discussion of the methods adopted and their success. Moreover, comment is required on the sharp contrast between a policy which denies to the price system the operation of its rationing function and one which relies primarily upon a restored free price system to maintain equilibrium through monetary and fiscal controls. The reluctance to use the policy of repressed inflation after 1950 arises in part from an awareness that it can be as damaging to the country's economic structure as an open inflation and from a realization that the drastic measures which repression suggests were not necessary.

In any study of the relative merits, differences and contrasts between a policy of repression and one employing primarily monetary and fiscal controls, it is necessary to recognize fully the importance of the economic setting in which each policy was adopted. As pointed out in Chapter I, World War II had destroyed about a quarter of the national wealth of Great Britain. Tremendous hardships had to be endured and great effort expended to restore the country to one of economic viability. It is to the great credit of the British people that in five short years a position of financial and economic balance had been attained.

Even if it is assumed that the new inflationary pressures beginning in 1950 were as strong as those which existed in the immediate post-war era, the effects that they would have on Britain's economy would be much different, for the economy in 1950 was far stronger than it was in 1945, and therefore more able to withstand any adverse economic events. However, granted the great difference in economic setting, there still exists a basis upon which a rough comparison and evaluation of the relative weaknesses and strengths of the two policies can be made.

The United Kingdom was approaching financial and economic balance in 1950 when the Korean conflict interrupted this orderly course of development and introduced fresh inflationary pressures into the economy. The effect of the conflict was to produce a severe balance-of-payments crisis in 1951-52. By the end of 1952 losses in gold and dollar reserves from June 30, 1951, had amounted to £780 million.[1]

It is important to separate the effects of the crisis on the United Kingdom from those on the rest of the sterling area. In the United Kingdom the favourable balance in 1950 was mainly due to the substantial reductions made in stocks of imported raw materials and foodstuffs which offset the worsening terms of trade. The running down of these stocks accounted for the simultaneous increase in monetary reserves.

The deterioration in the United Kingdom's balance of payments took place entirely in the second half of 1951. In the first half of 1951 the United Kingdom's current account deficit with all countries amounted to £93 million, in contrast with the deficit of £521 million in the second half.[2] The reasons for the deterioration in the United Kingdom's current payments position in the second half of 1951 were a sharp rise in import expenditure, a decline in invisible earnings and a fall in the volume of consumer goods exports. In addition to the current deficit, overseas investments increased by some £202 million, which imposed in part an additional drain on the gold and dollar reserves.

The sharp increase in import expenditures was required to replenish stocks, in particular the imports of raw materials and semi-manufactured products for use in industry. In real terms it is estimated that the volume of stocks in 1951 rose by £300 million.[3] The total import bill for 1951 was £1,092 million greater than in 1950. Higher prices accounted for two-thirds of

---

[1] *Economic Survey for 1953* (Cmd. 8800), p. 7.

[2] *Economic Survey for 1952* (Cmd. 8509), p. 9.

[3] Bank for International Settlements, *Twenty-Second Annual Report, 1st April 1951-31st March 1952*, Basle, June 9, 1952, p. 24.

the rise, the increase in import volume for the rest. Imports were about 16 per cent. greater in volume than in 1950. The increase in the volume of imports was only in small part offset by a 3 per cent. increase in exports.

The loss in invisible earnings, which amounted to £93 million in comparison with 1950, may be attributed in part to the Anglo-Iranian oil crisis resulting in the loss of the oil refineries at Abadan. Table III shows the changes which took place in the current account.

Table III

UNITED KINGDOM: CURRENT ACCOUNT OF THE BALANCE OF PAYMENTS

In millions of £ sterling

Items	1948	1949	1950	1951	1952	1953	1954*
Merchandise trade (f.o.b.):							
Imports . .	1,794	1,978	2,383	3,475	2,946	2,889	3,007
Exports and re-exports .	1,602	1,841	2,250	2,746	2,826	2,671	2,815
Balance of trade	−192	−137	−133	−729	−120	−218	−192
Invisible items (net):							
Interest, profits and dividends	+ 89	+ 94	+154	+125	+ 87	+ 59	+ 35
Shipping . .	+ 77	+ 91	+141	+139	+105	+124	+132
Travel . .	− 33	− 33	− 24	− 29	− 3	− 1	− 6
Government transactions .	− 76	−139	−136	−153	−172	−155	−169
Other items .	+136	+155	+298	+258	+241	+306	+310
Total of invisible items . .	+193	+168	+433	+340	+258	+333	+302
Total balance on current account	+ 1	+ 31	+300	−389	+138	+115	+110
Defence aid (net) .	—	—	—	+ 4	+121	+102	+ 50
Total balance including defence aid	+ 1	+ 31	+300	−385	+259	+217	+160

* Provisional figures.

Sources: Bank for International Settlements, *Twenty-Fourth Annual Report, 1st April 1953-31st March 1954*, Basle, June 14, 1954, p. 91, and ibid., *Twenty-Fifth Annual Report, 1st April 1954-31st March 1955*, Basle, June 13, 1955, p. 36.

H

As for the whole sterling area, its overseas members contributed as much to the swing in the area's gold and dollar balances as did the United Kingdom. The sharp rise in world commodity prices increased at first the foreign exchange reserves of the raw-material-producing countries of the sterling area. In the first half of 1951 their earnings more than offset the United Kingdom's deficit, and gold and dollar reserves increased by $567 million.[1] The large incomes generated by the heavy sales of raw materials resulted in doubling the rate of dollar imports in 1951 over 1950.

In the second half of 1951 foreign exchange earnings of the overseas members fell sharply as a result of the break in world commodity prices beginning in March 1951 and the reduction in the volume of imports of the United States. The decline in both commodity prices and United States' imports caused a 50 per cent. reduction in the dollar earnings of the overseas sterling area.[2] Since dollar imports lag behind the foreign exchange earnings, payments had to be made at a time when foreign exchange earnings were declining. As a result, members were forced to draw on the dollar pool in London to pay for imports.

It was the occurrence at the same time of the deficits of both the overseas members and the United Kingdom which produced the area's balance-of-payments crisis in 1951. The swing in the gold and dollar balances of the sterling area between 1950 and 1953 are given in Table IV.

If the earnings of the overseas members in the second half of 1951 had equalled their earnings in the first half, the payments crisis would not have developed. Over the whole of 1951 these countries showed little deficit, mostly spending in the second half their surpluses earned in the first half. In the first half of 1952 the United Kingdom's deficit was replaced by a small surplus, largely as a result of import controls. However, the deficit of the rest of the sterling area was continued and was not eliminated until the second half of 1952.

The Korean War unleased fresh inflationary pressures arising out of increased consumer and government expenditures. Consumers scrambled for goods which would become scarce in the event the conflict turned into a third world war. In terms of 1950 prices, personal consumption of food in the second half of 1950

[1] *Economic Survey for 1952* (Cmd. 8509), p. 9.
[2] *Op. cit.*, p. 11.

Table IV

UNITED KINGDOM AND REST OF THE STERLING AREA: GOLD AND DOLLAR BALANCE

Year	U.K. transactions with the dollar area				Rest of the sterling area: (including capital transactions with the dollar area and gold sales to U.K.)	Transactions with non-dollar areas[1]	Total balance in gold and dollars	
	Current Account not including defence aid	Defence aid	Other Transactions	Total				in millions of £ sterling
	in millions of U.S. dollars							
1950	− 245	—	+365	+ 120	+756	− 14	+ 862	+308
1951	−1,219	+ 11	−271	−1,479	+506	−167	−1,140	−407
1952	− 821	+338	− 94	− 389	+307	−407	− 487	−174
1953[2]	− 296	+286	+ 68	+ 58	+436	+178	+ 672	+240

[1] The largest item is constituted by the E.P.U. settlements in relation to the O.E.E.C. countries.
[2] Provisional figures.

Source: Bank for International Settlements, Twenty-Fourth Annual Report, 1st April 1953-31st March 1954, Basle, June 14, 1954, p. 90.

increased about 6 per cent., drink and tobacco about 13 per cent., clothing and durables about 20 per cent. and other goods and services about 7·6 per cent. As a result of increased consumer demand and the influence of world commodity prices the cost of living index rose 12 per cent., wholesale prices rose 29 per cent. and hourly wages 15 per cent. between June 1950 and December 1951.

Selected defence expenditures, which had amounted to £830 million in 1950-51, rose to £1,129 million in 1951-52,[1] converting an overall surplus of government revenue over expenditure of £247 million into an overall deficit of £150 million.[2] As can be seen, within two years the government account had deteriorated by £397 million.

The war also changed the pattern of industrial production. As shown in Table V, a pattern exists between the industrial production in November of the preceding year and the average

Table V

POST-WAR PATTERN OF INCREASES IN INDUSTRIAL PRODUCTION
(1946= 100)

	Year	November
1947	108	123
1948	121	129
1949	129	140
1950	140	153
1951	145	153

Source: Central Statistical Office, Monthly Digest of Statistics, H.M.S.O., London, January 1952.

production in the following year. According to this pattern industrial production in 1951 should have shown an index of 153. As can be seen, the average for 1951 was considerably below November 1950.

The drop in industrial production commenced in the autumn of 1951 with a sudden decline in the demand for consumer durables and semi-durables, particularly textiles. The decline in consumer demand was a reaction to heavy overbuying of textiles

[1] *Economic Survey for 1952* (Cmd. 8509), p. 20.

[2] Bank for International Settlements, *Twenty-Third Annual Report, 1st March 1952-31st March 1953*, Basle, June 8, 1953, p. 28.

and other consumer goods in the months immediately following the outbreak of the conflict. In addition, many overseas members of the sterling area faced with balance-of-payments difficulties arising out of the violent fluctuations in world commodity prices imposed import restrictions against the United Kingdom. Gross national product in real terms increased in 1951 by about 2·5 per cent. as compared to an increase of about 4·5 per cent. in 1949 and about 4 per cent. in 1950.[1]

The slump continued into 1952 and there was some fear of a general depression as unemployment rose. Gross national product for 1952 declined by 1·2 per cent. as compared to 1951. However, by the summer of 1952 the decline in the demand for textiles and footwear had come to an end. Demand rose slowly at first, but by the end of that year both production and employment in the affected industries had noticeably improved.

As a result of the inflationary pressures in 1951, the amount of dissaving in that year came to about £420 million, as indicated in Table VI. The increase in net investments between 1950 and 1951 of £769 million may be attributed to increased defence expenditures, a sharp rise in stocks and work in progress.

Table VI

UNITED KINGDOM: INVESTMENTS, SAVINGS AND THE BALANCE OF PAYMENTS

In millions of £ sterling

Items					1950	1951	1952
Total net savings	.	.	.	.	927	1,005	1,344
Total net investment	.	.	.	.	656	1,425	1,078
Difference	.	.	.	.	+271	−420	+266
Corresponding to current account of the balance of payments	.	.	.	.	+298	−398	+291
Receipts from disposal of wartime stocks, etc., abroad	.	.	.	.	− 27	− 22	− 25
Total	.	.	.	.	+271	−420	+266

Source: Bank for International Settlements: *Twenty-Third Annual Report, 1st April 1952-31st March 1953*, Basle, June 8, 1953, p. 59.

[1] Central Statistical Office, *National Income and Expenditure 1946-1953*, H.M.S.O., London, August 1954, p. 19.

The primary task facing the British government in 1952 was to stop the deterioration in its and the sterling area's balance-of-payments position. As was agreed at the Commonwealth Finance Ministers' meeting in January 1952, this was to be accomplished by the United Kingdom eliminating its deficit with the non-sterling world which had amounted to about £600 million in the latter half of 1951. Other members of the area were to increase exports to non-sterling countries and attain a surplus of £100 million in 1952.[1]

To carry out this programme the British government imposed severe import restrictions on food consumption and on stockpiling of food, tobacco and raw materials. It also reduced invisible expenditures on tourism, freights and government overseas expenditure.

With regard to the inflationary pressures, the government made a significant change in fiscal and monetary policy which reversed the policy of the previous years. The 1952-53 budget and the tax structure were redesigned to encourage incentives and output and to foster economic growth and promote flexibility in industry by redeployment of resources. In particular, the disincentive effects of high income taxation were recognized and changes made to induce greater labour effort by reducing the rates on overtime pay and promote personal savings.

A hard money policy was substituted for a cheap money policy, when the short-term discount rate on the London market was raised by the Bank of England from 2 to 2½ per cent. on November 8, 1951. Short-term rates had been pegged at 2 per cent. since October 1939. Long-term rates had been made flexible since the autumn of 1947. On March 4, 1952, to further tighten the money market short-term rates were raised to 4 per cent. Additional measures to restrain credit were: a decision by the Bank to hold itself free to supply cash to the market at its own discretion and not to freely purchase Treasury Bills from the market without limit at a fixed rate; a reduction in the floating debt; and the imposition of more qualitative controls.[2]

By far the most significant economic fact in 1952 was the

[1] *Economic Survey for 1952* (Cmd. 8509), p. 12.
[2] Bank for International Settlements, *Twenty-Second Annual Report, 1st April 1951-31st March 1952*, Basle, June 9, 1952, pp. 27-8.

amazing rise in personal savings of about 200 per cent. Gross personal savings were £102 million in 1950, £237 million in 1951, £706 million in 1952 and £870 million in 1953.[1] This sharp increase, which as already noted caused the temporary recession from the autumn of 1951 to the summer of 1952, is difficult to explain, aside from the influence of the changes in monetary and fiscal policy. It is probably not so much due to an increase in personal savings as to a decrease in personal dissaving as a result of the elimination of war-time involuntary savings and the end of personal restocking of consumer goods, which was aided by the check to the rise in prices and the realization that there was no longer any need to hurry to buy scarce items.

The direct effect of the credit change on the British balance of payments was the change in short and long-term capital movements. Increased confidence in sterling no longer made it worthwhile to delay sterling payments, and higher interest rates attracted investors both at home and abroad acting to reverse the outward flow of long-term capital. In the internal economy easier control over the cash and liquidity position of commercial banks induced a change in lending policies. Bank advances and deposits declined—the first downward movement in many years —and a considerable change-over from current to time deposits occurred. Although the gross national product in money terms expanded 9 per cent. and the cost of living in 1952 rose 6 per cent., the restrictive credit policies prevented any significant increase in the money supply.[2]

The elimination of the excessive money supply coupled with a decline in world commodity prices, which had reached their peak on or about March 15, 1951, made possible the restoration of many of the free commodity markets without endangering the country's monetary reserves.[3] Falling world commodity

[1] Central Statistical Office, *National Income and Expenditure 1946-1953*, London, H.M.S.O., August 1954, p. 5.

[2] Bank for International Settlements, *Twenty-Third Annual Report, 1st April 1952-31st March 1953*, Basle, June 8, 1953, p. 25.

[3] The first commodity market to be reopened was the rubber market in November 1946. Coffee followed in July 1947, tin in November 1949, cocoa in January 1951, lead in October 1952, raw sugar in November 1952, zinc in January 1953, copper in August 1953 and cotton in May 1954. Bank for International Settlements, *Twenty-Fourth Annual Report, 1st April 1953-31st March 1954*, Basle, June 14, 1954, p. 40.

prices increased supplies, and with the easing of consumer demand rationing all but came to an end by the summer of 1954, butter and fats having been freed in May and meat in July 1954.

A return to flexible price and cost relationships was aided by the reopening of many of the pre-World War II markets for staple commodities. Other governmental decisions reflecting the same determination to return to more normal marketing conditions were the opening of the foreign exchange market in December 1951 and the gold market in March 1954. The improvement in the world confidence in sterling may be noted by the fact that American Account sterling was being quoted above par in 1953 and 1954, and Transferable Account sterling in March 1954 had been quoted at $2·78 and above.

The strain on the British and sterling area balance of payments which had occurred in 1951 and 1952 was overcome by 1953. In 1953 value of imports fell by £532 million below the value of 1952. The improvement in Britain's trade balance may be attributed to the contraction in the volume of imports because of increased restrictions, the return to balanced internal conditions caused by the passing of inflation, an increase in the volume of exports and an improvement in the terms of trade. In terms of volume in 1953, Britain imported 9 per cent. more goods at a cost 4 per cent. less than in 1952.[1] In line with the government's decision to return to more normal marketing conditions foodstuffs and manufactured articles were placed on open general licence in March 1953.

The improvement in Britain's external position was reflected in growing production at home and an increase in personal consumption expenditures and savings. Gross domestic product in real terms rose about 4 per cent. over 1952. Industrial production was about 6 per cent. above the level reached in 1951.[2] Moreover, there was such a marked improvement in output per man in 1953 that an increase of 6 per cent. in the total wage and salary bill did not cause a significant rise in labour costs per unit of output.[3]

As a result of increased production in 1953, personal dispos-

[1] Bank for International Settlements, *Twenty-Fourth Annual Report, 1st April 1953-31st March 1954*, Basle, June 14, 1954, p. 92.
[2] *Economic Survey for 1954* (Cmd. 9108), p. 18.
[3] *Op. cit.*, p. 30.

able income increased about 7 per cent. Since retail prices for consumer goods during 1953 increased about 3 per cent., an expansion in consumption could take place without any reduction in personal savings. The striking growth in personal savings reflected greater confidence in the currency, in stability of price-cost relationships and in the availability of supplies.

Beginning in the autumn of 1954, new inflationary pressures appeared once again in the economy of the United Kingdom and produced the familiar pattern of a balance-of-payments deficit. These new pressures, which have continued into 1955, arose primarily from a condition of 'brim-full' employment, a sharp increase in consumer goods purchases, rising wage rates and high levels of real investment. To counteract these pressures, the government continued to rely primarily on monetary policy: Bank Rate was raised in February 1955 to $4\frac{1}{2}$ per cent., sterner hire-purchase requirements were adopted, and tighter credit controls were imposed on commercial bank advances.

Had the government adopted a policy of repression to combat the inflationary pressures since 1950, it is doubtful whether the high production levels for these years would have been attained. As has already been shown in Chapter III, factor allocation hinders production and increases costs. It is doubtful under repressed inflation that the expected production increase of 5 to 6 per cent. in 1955 over 1954 could have been attained with the occurrence of a seven-week dock and a three-week railway strike, for factor controls would not have permitted the optimum distribution of scarce resources to maintain production. Moreover, it is of interest that the continuing high level of production has been maintained with stocks of raw materials and other resources at no higher level in relation to total national output than in some of the years of repressed inflation.[1]

In summary, attention must be brought to the success the new monetary and fiscal policies had in stimulating savings, helping to reduce consumption and rather quickly restoring viability to the balance of payments and the economy. It is impossible to prove that had similar policies been adopted soon after World War II it would have been successful in restoring flexibility and viability to the British economy at a date earlier than 1950.

[1] Cf. 'By Hard Money Alone', *The Economist*, Vol. CLXXVI, No. 5838, July 16, 1955, p. 199.

However, the success such policies had in reducing the supply of money and restoring confidence in savings suggests that many of the evils of repressed inflation might have been lessened or perhaps altogether avoided if such policies had been adopted.

Index

Printed in the United States
by Baker & Taylor Publisher Services